TROUT FISHING *in* SHETLAND

Printed and published by
The Shetland Times Ltd.
Lerwick

Published by The Shetland Times Ltd., 1998.

ISBN 1 898852 37 5

British Library Cataloguing-in-Publication Data
A catalogue record for this book is
available from the British Library.

Printed and published by
The Shetland Times Ltd.,
Prince Alfred Street, Lerwick,
Shetland ZE1 0EP.

Contents

Foreword

The last angling guide to be produced by the Shetland Anglers' Association was published in 1982 and it was felt that some of the information had become outdated and that a new guide was needed.

This new booklet, which is designed primarily to assist the visiting angler, gives information on almost two hundred of Shetland's main lochs.

Thanks go to members of the Association who gave willingly of their knowledge, and also to the Whalsay Angling Club and the Unst Angling Club for their assistance. Thanks also to Richard Stafford for his design work and the following for use of photographs: Peter Gathercole; Graeme Callandar; Richard Stafford; Keiran Murray; David Fullerton and Brian Hunter, and finally to Alan Johnson for his time and effort spent compiling this booklet.

Graeme Callander
President
1998

THE SHETLAND ISLANDS

So often relegated to a small box in the Moray Firth, it is little wonder that many people on the British mainland have little idea of the exact location of the islands. That changed somewhat with the discovery of oil in the waters east of Shetland in the 1970's when the large Sullom Voe terminal was built in the isles.

Shetland is, in fact, a group of about one hundred islands lying between 60 and 61 degrees north but the angler will be interested in only the largest six - Mainland, Yell, Unst, Fetlar, Whalsay and Bressay. One advantage which the northerly location of the isles brings is the long hours of daylight; the simmer dim, when in midsummer there is no proper darkness and the angler can fish through the night if he wishes.

TRAVEL: The visiting angler has a choice of two methods to reach the isles: either by plane from one of the major Scottish airports or by P&O ferry from Aberdeen. Accommodation is available throughout most of the islands and details can be obtained from Shetland Islands Tourism's Lerwick office (tel: 01595 693434).

Easy access to most lochs but some hill lochs require a trek.

Public transport is limited but car hire is available throughout the islands. Inter island drive-on, drive-off vehicle ferries operate a frequent service between Mainland and the islands of Bressay, Whalsay, Yell, Unst and Fetlar.

Lerwick is the island's capital and houses about a third of the island's population of approximately 22,000. The town owes it's existence to the sheltered harbour which for centuries has served as a safe haven for a number of fishing fleets, both British and foreign, and in more recent times the oil-related vessels associated with the North Sea oilfields.

CLIMATE: The climate is remarkably temperate considering the latitude; the warm seas and the gulf stream ensuring that there are few extremes. The normal average monthly temperatures and rainfall for January are 3° C and 110mm, and for July they are 12° C and 65mm. Weather conditions can change very quickly, whether summer or winter, and there are times when one side of the islands can be in bright sunshine whilst the other has thick fog. One thing which is almost always present is the wind though gales are rare during the summer months.

The simmer dim - ideal long fishing nights of Shetland's summer.

THE SHETLAND ANGLERS' ASSOCIATION

The Association was formed in 1920 and has, over the years, done much to improve the fishing, both for brown trout and sea trout. It owns certain fishing rights outright, and rents or has permission to fish on most of the other mainland fishings. The SAA runs fishing competitions throughout the season and a list of these will be issued when you buy your reasonably priced permit.

FISHING PERMITS: Permits can be purchased at either the Lerwick Tourist Office or the tackle shop, Rod and Line, which is in Harbour Street in Lerwick.You will also recieve a map and list of rules concerning the restrictions on the loch of Spiggie which is owned by the RSPB and is rented by the SAA.The Association also has a number of boats for hire to members and visitors and details of these can be obtained from the tackle shop.

STOCKING PROGRAMME: Over the years many of the more popular lochs have been periodically stocked with brown trout and in 1995 the Association embarked on a comprehensive stocking programme involving up to 80,000 fish per annum (mostly fry of about 1"), aided by grants from the Shetland Islands Council, Shetland Enterprise and EC funds. A number of sea trout locations have also been stocked recently in an attempt to encourage a revival of Shetland's once famous migratory trout stocks.

CLUBHOUSE: Apart from pursuing actively its policy of developing Shetland trout and sea trout angling facilities in general, the SAA also owns a licensed clubhouse to which visiting anglers are welcome. Hours of opening are from eight pm to eleven pm on Tuesdays and Fridays.

Association boats are available for hire on five local lochs.

Boats at Benston Loch.

GAME FISH SPECIES

BROWN TROUT: Season 15th March-6th October.
The wild brown trout range from an average of 10 ounces to fish of more than five pounds - the largest in recent times being a fish of 9 pounds 4 ounces.

SEA TROUT: Season 25th February-31st October.
Sea trout can be caught in a number of lochs where the fish have access from the sea, though it is usually August or September before they enter fresh water. Most sea trout are caught in salt water, both on fly and spinner, when the fish gather at the burn mouths in the autumn.

SALMON: Season 25th February-31st October.
Small numbers of salmon, both wild fish and escapees from fish farms, are found in the voes and burns later in the year and the occasional fish is taken.

CHAR: Season 15th March-6th October.
The only other game fish in Shetland is the char which is found in the Loch of Girlsta and these can occasionally be caught on the fly during the summer months. The Association have a policy of returning all char to the water.

Wild trout from Tingwall Loch.

Shetland wild salmon.

FISHING EQUIPMENT AND METHODS

FLY FISHING: A carbon rod of about 10 feet in length rated for a line AFTM No. 6 to 8 would be perfectly adequate for Shetland lochs though some would prefer a slightly longer rod for boat fishing. Floating lines are the most commonly used, both double taper and weight forward, though a sinking line can be useful at times when the trout are lying deeper.

FLY PATTERNS: The most frequently used flies on the Shetland lochs are the traditional loch flies, usually fished two or three to a cast. Sizes 10, 12 and 14 are the norm but in a good wind a size 8 fished on or close to the surface can bring the fish up. In the early season the darker flies work best: Black Zulu, Bibio, Kate McLaren for the bob; Mallard and Claret, Black Ke-He, Connemara for the middle and a Black Pennel or small Ace of Spades on the tail. As the water warms up and fly life increases other patterns can be added: Greenwell's Glory, Coachman, Clan Chief, Invicta and the Loch Ordie. Nymphal patterns can be effective especially when the air is cold and the fish are loath to come to the surface and the following would be worth trying: Gold-Bead Hare's Ear, Buzzer nymphs (black is most common) and Pheasant Tail Nymph. Other successful flies would include: Ke-He, Extractor, March Brown, Soldier Palmer, Wickham's and a number of T. C. Kingsmill Moore's Bumbles including the Golden Olive Bumble and Claret Bumble.

BAIT FISHING: Although not actively opposed to worm fishing the SAA policy has been not to favour this type of fishing for conservation reasons. Float fishing or static ledgering tends to lead to the deep hooking of fish which greatly reduces the chances of returning undersized fish safely to the water.

SPINNING: While the Association is keen to promote fly fishing as much as possible, spinning is allowed on most of the lochs but two exceptions are the lochs of Spiggie and Benston. A seven or eight foot rod is adequate with a 6 to 8 pound line. Favourite lures are Mepps and Toby. Spinning can produce the bigger fish - especially in the early months of the season.

BANK FISHING: With only a few of the larger roadside lochs accessible to the boat angler, bank fishing is the most common method of taking fish. For many of the lochs a pair of waders are essential as the fish may be well out from the bank but the shallow water should be fished first as fish will come close in to feed especially early and late in the day. Shallow water can also be productive early in the season as it warms up faster than the deeper parts of the loch

A selection of tried and tested flies and spinners.

attracted to the increased insect life in the warmer water. The angler who intends to walk a few miles to fish the more remote hill lochs may find a pair of wellies or walking boots more comfortable. Many of these lochs have deeper water close to shore and wading is unnecessary.

Casting with the wind behind may be easiest but is not always the most productive - bringing the flies in across the wind seems to be more effective and the retrieve should be varied; sometimes a slow figure of eight is best and at other times a fast retrieve can work. It is best to experiment with the retrieve until the fish let you know which method they prefer.

Wading on Clings Water.

BOAT FISHING: The most commonly used method is the traditional 'Scottish loch style'; that is, drifting side-on to the wind and the angler fishing the water in front of the boat. Most of the action will be found over the shallower areas of the loch and areas around weed beds. If you can find a part of the loch where the wind is blowing parallel along the shore all the better as a long drift can be had over productive water before having to motor back up the loch to start the next drift. Drifting onto the windward shore is also an effective way of catching fish, which can sometimes be found very close in, sometimes in less than a foot of water. This is a slightly hazardous tactic as the danger of running ashore is high if the outboard motor doesn't start. Outboard motors can be used on most of Shetland's lochs but one notable exception is Spiggie Loch which is owned by the RSPB.

Even in the summer the days can be cool and anglers are well advised to wear plenty of warm and waterproof clothing as the weather can change very quickly. A bouyancy aid of some sort is also an essential item in case of accidents, far too many anglers have drowned because they weren't wearing one. Finally, try to remain seated in the boat, many anglers are to be seen standing up and fishing but this has led to many an angler losing balance and ending up in the water.

Fishing the shore line – Benston Loch.

FLOAT TUBING: Float Tubing, Belly Boating, call it what you will, the many lochs on the Shetland Isles with no restrictions on their use make these islands a paradise for this method of angling. Although originally developed in the United States to give anglers access to steep sided river gorges where wading was impossible they have found a place in the armoury of wild trout anglers in Shetland. Used as a miniature boat, the float tube allows the angler to fish the many hill lochs where access for boats is impossible and where bank fishing has been the only method possible to date.

With carrying straps and a large number of pockets for tackle on the float tube the angler can hike for up to an hour into the hills and cover virgin water, fishing around islands, skerries and weed beds that have never been fished due to the inaccessibility for boats. The single angler can also fish closer to these hot spots, holding position comfortably, whereas, a boat would drift over these areas too quickly.

Due to the northern latitude of the islands, water temperature can be a bit on the cool side all year round so neoprene chest waders are recommended although rubber or PVC chest waders can be used with thermal or fleeced lined underwear. Lack of suitable protection can lead to severe cramps, and since your legs are your only method of propulsion, this can leave you sitting adrift in the middle of a loch at the mercy of the wind.

Trout often rise within touching distance of the float tube, therefore rods as short as eight feet can be used successfully although many local anglers use their normal boat rods.

For safety it is recommended that a buoyancy aid or inflatable life jacket is worn when float tubing. Although it is extremely difficult to capsize a float tube due to the low centre of gravity, it is possible to puncture the main buoyancy membrane with a hook. A punctured main membrane will not burst with a bang, but will deflate slowly, and a life jacket together with the float tube's secondary membranes will allow the angler to reach the safety of the bank from the middle of a loch.

Float tubing on Spiggie Loch.

A few local anglers have used their float tubes with success in winds up to 40 knots, waves crashing about their ears, but this isn't advisable for newcomers to this method of angling. Apart from being a touch uncomfortable, it can be extremely tiring on the legs trying to hold station or controlling your drift.

For those anglers wishing to try this method for the first time, Rod and Line tackle shop has a float tube for hire and can arrange for novice float tubers to be accompanied by an experienced local.

THE TROUT'S ENVIRONMENT

In the past Shetland was famous for its large runs of sea trout, some of which ran to ten pounds or more and were fished for mainly at the heads of the voes or sea lochs or anywhere where the freshwater burns entered the sea. This was where the sea trout shoals would congregate waiting for a spate to give them access to the streams and lochs. The season for the sea trout was a long one; from early February to the end of October, but during the middle of the season the sea trout tended to lie further offshore and were therefore unavailable to the angler fishing from the shore, and during the months of June and July anglers looking for some sport had to resort to fishing the lochs for the brown trout.

Unfortunately sea trout fishing in the isles has seen a drastic decline over recent years and consequently the angling pressure on the freshwater lochs has increased and the vast majority of anglers in Shetland now concentrate on brown trout fishing. Most of the lochs contain trout though there is a large variation in size ranging from a few ounces up to many pounds. A number of things can affect the size and abundance of fish in a loch and these include the availability of good spawning burns, the underlying geology which can have a great effect on the fertility of the loch (the bands of limestone running north/south through the Shetland mainland being particularly important), and the amount of food available to the fish. Man can also have an effect - the application of fertiliser or slurry on farmland around the lochs may increase the alkalinity or richness of the water running off the land into the loch. In the case of an acid loch with little food for the trout this runoff may actually improve the fishing and size of the trout. Where it affects an already fertile loch the effect may be more serious with the added growth of weed and, in warm weather the growth of green or brown algae which in extreme cases can turn the loch an unnatural green colour.

Typical hill lochs of the North Mainland.

Clousta Loch - West Mainland.

Shetland has at least 400 trout lochs ranging in size from less than an acre to the large valley trough lochs of Girlsta and Cliff. Many of the lochs lie in areas with extensive peat cover and the rainwater running off the moor into the lochs can seriously affect their fertility. This runoff from the peat produces brown-tinged water which is both acid and nutrient-poor and is usually home to small, dark trout. Also many lochs are to be found in hollows in the base rock gouged out by the thick ice sheets which covered Shetland during the colder episodes of our history. Most of the lochs within a mile of the sea are, to a greater or lesser degree, affected by salt spray. Frequent gales during the winter months mean some lochs closest to the sea, even though not directly connected with it, could almost be described as brackish.

Compared to the rest of Britain the isles have a high average wind speed with the result that Shetland lochs are significantly affected by wave action. As a consequence there are few areas of sheltered shoreline where aquatic plants can colonise and survive and most shorelines are either wavewashed rocks, shingle or sand.

For its size Shetland has a wide variation of loch types, the five most important are as follows:

	No of lochs	% of total
DYSTROPHIC	547	34.7
OLIGOTROPHIC	661	41.9
MESOTROPHIC	212	13.4
EUTROPHIC	111	7.0
BRACKISH	45	2.8

(figures from the NCC 1974)

DYSTROPHIC: lochs are mainly small, nutrient-poor and basically nothing more than a hole in the peat filled with water. These "dubh lochans" are soft edged and are of little interest to anglers as the vast majority hold no fish. They are often used by nesting red throated divers.

Fishing Spiggie Loch in the early spring.

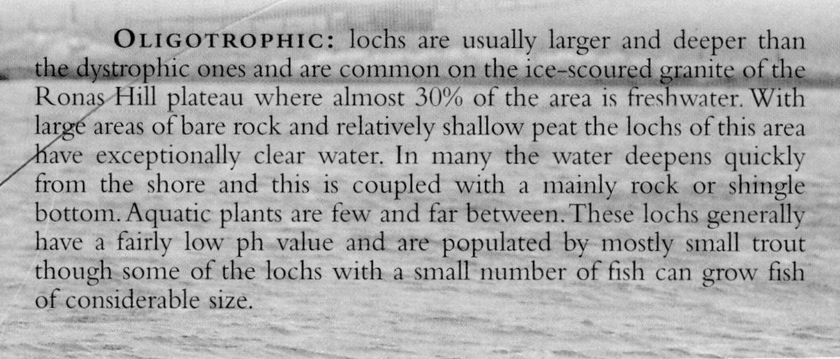

OLIGOTROPHIC: lochs are usually larger and deeper than the dystrophic ones and are common on the ice-scoured granite of the Ronas Hill plateau where almost 30% of the area is freshwater. With large areas of bare rock and relatively shallow peat the lochs of this area have exceptionally clear water. In many the water deepens quickly from the shore and this is coupled with a mainly rock or shingle bottom. Aquatic plants are few and far between. These lochs generally have a fairly low ph value and are populated by mostly small trout though some of the lochs with a small number of fish can grow fish of considerable size.

MESOTROPHIC: lochs lie on relatively basic rocks, commonly hard sandstones, as in the west mainland. Though these lochs may be little more productive than the former some of the mesotrophic lochs lie on limestone and these can hold good stocks of quality trout. These also have a larger variety of aquatic plants and in some of these lochs fishing can be difficult due to the prolific weed growth which can occur in the late summer.

EUTROPHIC: lochs are mainly small with the notable exception of Spiggie Loch and are the most fertile type with good plant growth and a high ph value.

BRACKISH: lochs are also generally small with the exception of Strom Loch which is more than a mile long. Some of these lochs have a high enough concentration of salt water to encourage the growth of seaweed and may also contain species of marine fish such as coalfish and flounder and are important to the angler who has an interest in catching the sea trout which are often found in them.

Birka Water.

The streams and burns are mainly small and have only small brown trout though the few larger burns like the Laxo Burn, Weisdale Burn and the Arisdale burn in Yell had large runs of sea trout and also small numbers of salmon most of which were under 10 pounds in weight.

Loch of Huxter - Whalsay.

Selecting the right fly.

THE TROUT'S MENU

The Shetland trout's menu is wide and varied ranging from sticklebacks and the fry of it's own species to the tiniest of insects. In order to achieve success, the fly-fisherman should have at least a rudimentary knowledge of these food items and how to imitate them.

The main food items are insects, especially those which spend part of their lives living in the water as larvae before rising to the surface to hatch into adults.

For simplicity most of these insects can be arranged into three groups as following;-

Spooning can help your choice of fly.

1. THE UPWINGED FLIES or Ephemeroptera

To date six species of these flies have been found in Shetland, one of which is very small and difficult to imitate. All these flies spend most of their lives in the water and when adult have a segmented body, two or three long tails and large upright transparent wings. A number of these flies have a grey/green body and a good general purpose fly to imitate these is the old pattern, the Greenwell's Glory.

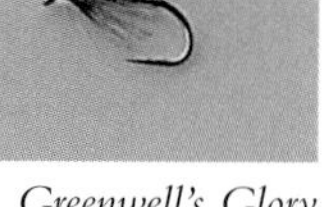

Greenwell's Glory

GREENWELL'S GLORY

Tying thread	olive
Body	green-olive seals fur
Rib	fine oval gold tinsel
Hackle	greenwell hen
Wings	grey starling or mallard

The body of the fly should be slim and a tail of yellow floss is sometimes added to this pattern. This pattern without the wings and tied more sparsly is the Greenwell Spider and fished slower and deeper is a fair imitation of the nymphal stage of the fly.

Another couple of patterns worth trying are as follows;

Rough Olive

ROUGH OLIVE

Tying silk	olive
Tail	olive cock hackle fibres
Rib	oval gold tinsel
Body	heron herl dyed olive
Hackle	medium olive cock
Wing	grey starling or mallard

GOLDEN OLIVE

Tying silk	olive or brown
Tail	golden pheasant topping
Rib	fine oval gold tinsel
Body	golden olive seals fur
Hackle	olive or light ginger cock
Wing	bronze mallard

2. THE FLAT-WINGED FLIES or Diptera

This is a large order of insects, which includes all the true flies and is larger than all the other orders put together. They have two rather short transparent wings which lie flat along the top of the body and have no tails. Most of the flies in this order which are of interest to anglers are aquatic and can be divided into three main groups - crane flies, terrestrial flies and midges, the latter being the most important to the fly fisher.

The crane flies, generally known as Daddy Longlegs, are commonly found on most lochs especially in the second half of the summer. A poor flier, it is easily blown onto the water even by the lightest of breezes. Some pass their larval stage in damp ground and others in shallow water. These are large ungainly insects and make a good mouthful for the trout. Some anglers imitate these flies by dapping a large bushy fly in front of a drifting boat or occasionally from the shore if there is enough wind.

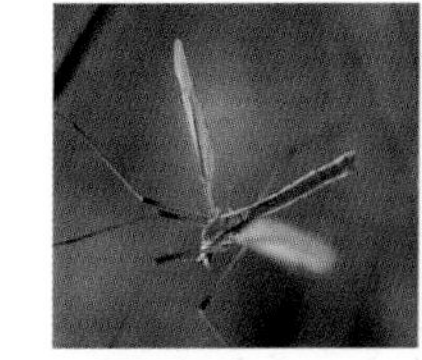

Crane fly

DADDY LONGLEGS (dry)

Hook	size 10 longshank
Tying silk	black
Rib	fine oval gold tinsel
Body	natural raffia (moistened)
Legs	six cock pheasant centre tail fibres, knotted once
Wing	badger hackle points
Hackle	red game cock

WET DADDY

Hook	size 10 longshank
Tying silk	black
Rib	fine oval gold tinsel
Body	dirty-yellow floss
Body hackle	red game cock
Hackle	golden pheasant tippet feather tied long

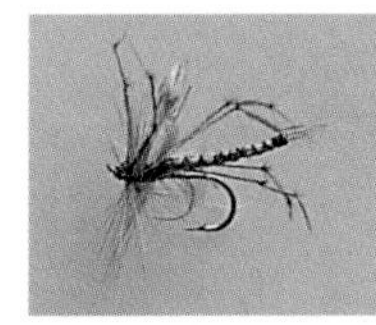

Daddy Longlegs

Early season fish - Clings Water Loch.

Midge pupa

As stated earlier the midges are an important food item to the trout and most spend their larval and pupal stages in the water. Often called buzzers by anglers hatches of these flies occur during most of the fishing season and they can be found in almost all of Shetland's lochs. The densest hatches occur in the evening or early morning though in fine weather flies will hatch at any time of day. They vary greatly in size from the small biting variety to some of about 10mm in length. Black is the commonest colour though some are green or orange. The larvae live on the bottom of the loch until they pupate when they make their way to the surface to hatch into the adult fly. This is the time when they are most vulnerable to the trout. There is a wide selection of artificials to imitate both pupa and adult stages.

Black Pennell

BLACK MIDGE PUPA

Tying silk	black
Tail	a few white hackle fibres - short
Rib	fine copper wire
Body	bronze peacock herl - thin and tied well round the hook bend
Wing cases	crow wing fibres
Thorax	as for the body
Breathers	small tuft of white wool

BLACK PENNELL

Tying silk	black
Tail	golden pheasant tippet
Rib	fine oval silver tinsel
Body	black floss
Hackle	black cock - two turns only

A couple of traditional patterns imitating the adult midge are as follows:

Connemara Black

CONNEMARA BLACK

Tying silk	black
Tail	golden pheasant topping
Rib	fine oval silver tinsel
Body	black seals fur
Hackle	black cock or hen with blue jay tied at throat
Wing	bronze mallard

BLAE AND BLACK

Tying silk	black
Rib	fine oval silver tinsel
Body	black floss
Hackle	black hen
Wing	grey starling or mallard

Two flies which one would not normally consider using during a buzzer hatch which work well are: Teal, Blue & Silver and a Coachman

Teal, Blue and Silver

TEAL, BLUE AND SILVER

Tying silk	black
Tail	golden pheasant tippet
Rib	fine oval silver tinsel
Body	flat silver tinsel
Hackle	light blue hen
Wing	teal

COACHMAN

Tying silk	black
Body	peacock herl
Hackle	red game hen
Wing	white mallard feather

Of the terrestrial flies the heather fly and the dung fly are probably the most important. The heather fly hatches out from the heather in the second half of the summer and being a poor flyer it quite often gets blown onto the loch. A good imitation of this insect is the Bloody Doctor though any fly incorporating black and red, the Bibio for instance, would do.

BLOODY DOCTOR

Tying silk	black
Rib	fine copper wire
Body	black ostrich herl
Wings	grey mallard
Hackles	red cock followed by a black cock - both in front of the wings

BIBIO

Tying silk	black
Rib	oval silver tinsel
Body	in three parts - black-red-black seals fur
Hackle	black cock - palmered

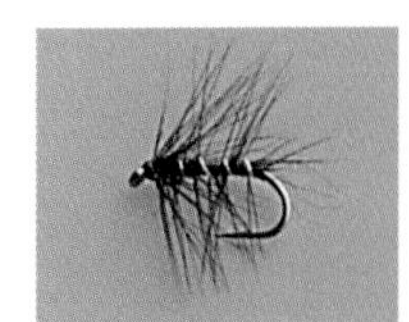

Bibio

COWDUNG

Tying silk	black
Rib	gold oval tinsel
Body	olive seals fur
Wing	goose shoulder feather dyed cinnamon
Hackle	ginger cock

COCH Y BONDDU

Tying silk	black
Tag	flat gold tinsel
Body	peacock herl
Rib	fine gold tinsel
Hackle	furnace hen

Cowdung

3. FLIES WITH ROOF-SHAPED WINGS or Trichoptera

These are the sedges or caddis-flies and spend most of their lives in the water where the larva makes itself a case of sand or vegetable matter in which it lives for protection during the underwater stage of its life. Though looking very much like moths the sedges wings lie along the body in an inverted V-shape whereas the moths wings lie flat.

Caddis larva

Like the moths many sedges are nocturnal, hatching out in the evening as the light begins to fade though some do hatch during the day. The trout will take the larvae at any time of the season though the adult flies only emerge during the second half of the season from the end of May onwards in Shetland and it is at this time that the trout will take the ascending pupae or the adult on the surface before it takes off.

Adult sedge

The adult flies vary greatly in colour and size from the small to medium black sedges to the larger cinnamon sedge and mottled sedge to the largest of them all the great red sedge. There are a great many patterns both old and new to imitate the sedge and a few are given here.

Invicta

INVICTA

Tying silk	brown
Tail	golden pheasant topping
Rib	fine oval gold tinsel
Body	amber seals fur
Hackle	red game cock - palmered, beard hackle blue jay
Wings	hen pheasant centre tail

BLACK SPECKLED SEDGE

Tying silk	black
Rib	silver oval tinsel
Body	black seals fur
Body hackle	black cock
Wing	speckled-brown hen wing quill
Head hackle	black cock

Wickham's Fancy

GOLD-BEAD SEDGE PUPA

Tying silk	brown
Rib	fine oval gold tinsel
Body	amber seals fur
Thorax	dark brown seals fur
Head	small gold-bead

WICKHAM'S FANCY

Tying silk	brown
Tails	red game hackle fibres
Rib	oval gold tinsel
Body	flat gold tinsel
Hackle	palmered red game cock
Wings	grey mallard

Some sedges have a pale green body and a useful fly to represent these is the Green Peter whilst what is probably the most popular fly in Shetland, the Loch Ordie is almost certainly taken for a sedge either fished as a wet fly on the bob or dipped in floatant and skated across the surface.

Loch Ordie

GREEN PETER

Tying silk	brown
Rib	fine oval gold tinsel
Body	green olive seals fur
Wings	hen pheasant secondary feather
Hackle	red game cock tied in front of the wing

LOCH ORDIE

Body	as many red-brown cock hackles as the hook shank will hold leaving room for one or two white cock hackles at the head

Whilst this list covers the main food items in the Shetland lochs there are others such as the freshwater shrimp and sticklebacks and in some lochs the freshwater snail is important. Shetland anglers rarely fish with specific imitations of these though undoubtedly they can be an important part of the trout's diet at times. Daphnia, also called the water flea, can be common during the warmer months and trout can sometimes take large quantities of this tiny crustacean. A brightly coloured fly is said to be worth a try at this time.

Shetland Anglers' Association member Graeme Callander is particularly interested in the study of the trout's diet and the following information and graph show the results of his work;

This review was compiled with the help of the experts - the trout themselves. The stomach contents of 146 Shetland trout were analysed and the findings are presented here.

Month	No. of trout	Food source followed by the number of fish that had eaten the source
March	4	Stickleback 1, cased caddis 1, shrimp 1, stonefly nymph 1.
April	13	Cased caddis 7, shrimp 6, midge pupa 5, snail 5, stickleback 1.
May	33	Shrimp 14, cased caddis 13, stickleback 10, snail 10, midge larvae 4, daphnia 4, midge pupa 3
June	31	Cased caddis 11, snail 9, shrimp 8, midge pupa 8, stickleback 6, daphnia 5, midge larva 4, corixa 3, sedge pupa 3, terrestrials 2, adult sedge 1.
July	36	Midge pupa 15, sedge pupa 13, shrimp 10, snail 10, daphnia 7, terrestrials 7, cased caddis 6, caenis nymph 5, midge larva 4, adult sedge 3, mayfly nymph 3, stickleback 3, corixa 2, diving beetle 1, aquatic beetle 1, adult midge 1, caseless caddis 1, beetle larva 1, pea mussel 1.
Aug.	18	Midge pupa 7, stickleback 5, sedge pupa 5, adult sedge 2, snail 2, shrimp 1, daddy long legs 1.
Sept.	11	Sticklebacks 9, snail 4, shrimp 1.

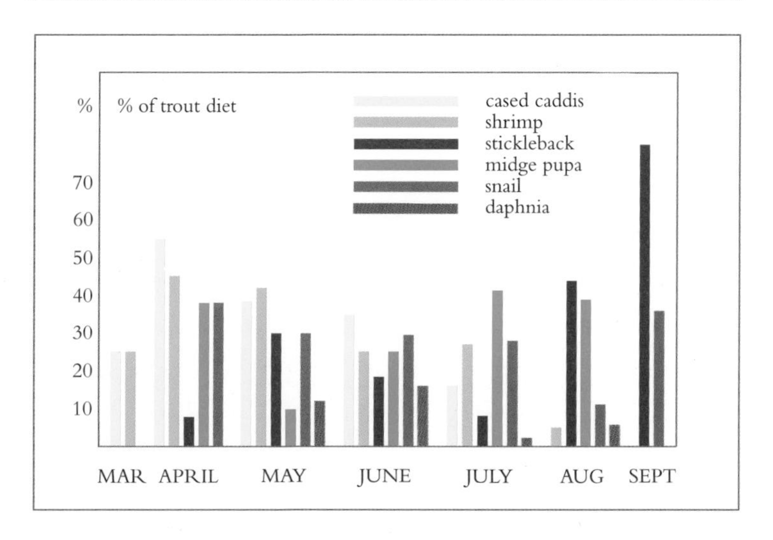

By way of an explanation and to help understand the table better:

- All types of cased caddis were grouped together, but the most common type eaten by the trout in the survey were the sand-cased caddis up to 1cm long.
- All types of sedge pupa were grouped together ranging from small 5mm brown and yellow to 15mm brown and green.
- All types of adult sedge were grouped together, as were the adult midge and midge larvae.
- The most common colours of midge pupa were olive, black and brown.
- The most common type of terrestrial found in the stomach of those trout surveyed was similar to a housefly, but land beetles were also grouped in this catagory. It was felt that although terrestrials, daddy long legs and ants were a special case and should be recorded separately.
- The diving beetle was a Great Diving Beetle eaten by a 2lb Foula trout, while other diving beetles recorded were much smaller.
- Mayfly nymphs were of the agile darter type.

Gold Invicta

Over the years the "traditional wet flies" have been the mainstay of the Shetland angler's armoury and whilst today many brown trout are still caught on them some of the more modern flies and tactics are now employed. The following list of patterns, some traditional and some less well known, have been proven as being effective and along with all the flies previously mentioned will give the visiting angler some guidance as to the artificials which he or she would find useful.

Bruiser

GOLD INVICTA

Tying silk	brown
Tail	golden pheasant topping
Rib	fine oval gold tinsel
Body	flat gold tinsel
Hackle	red game palmered
Wing	hen pheasant centre tail

BRUISER

Tying silk	black
Tail	light blue floss
Rib	oval silver tinsel
Body	light blue seals fur
Hackles	blue and black cock wound together

Amber Dabbler

OLIVE DABBLER

Tying silk	black
Tails	cock pheasant fibres
Rib	oval gold tinsel
Body	olive seals fur
Hackle	olive cock palmered
Wing	bronze mallard tied to cloak the fly

AMBER DABBLER

Tying silk	black
Tails	cock pheasant fibres
Rib	oval gold tinsel
Body	amber seals fur
Hackle	red game palmered
Wing	bronze mallard tied to cloak the fly

CLAN CHIEF

Tying silk	black
Tag	two turns flat silver
Tail	scarlet floss on top of yellow floss
Body	black seals fur
Rib	oval silver tinsel
Body hackle	red and black cock wound together
Head hackle	black hen

EXTRACTOR

Tying silk	black
Tail	a pinch of golden pheasant red body feather
Rib	oval gold tinsel
Body	flat gold tinsel
Head hackle	yellow cock with a red game cock in front
Wing	bronze mallard

Clan Chief

EDDIE'S FAVOURITE

Tying silk	black
Rib	oval gold tinsel
Body	black ostrich herl
Body hackle	furnace cock
Head hackle	furnace cock or hen

SOLDIER PALMER

Tying silk	brown
Tail	red wool
Rib	oval gold tinsel
Body	red seals fur
Hackle	red game palmered

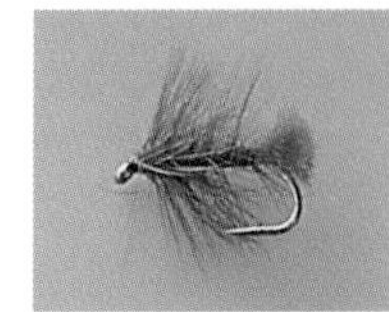

Soldier Palmer

BLACK ZULU

Tying silk	black
Tail	red wool
Rib	oval silver tinsel
Body	black seals fur
Hackle	black cock palmered

GREEN TAG ZULU

Tying silk	black
Tail	bright green floss
Body	black seals fur
Rib	oval silver tinsel
Hackle	black cock palmered

Green Tag Zulu

BLUE ZULU

Tying silk	black
Tail	red wool
Rib	oval silver tinsel
Body	black seals fur
Hackle	black cock palmered
Head hackle	blue cock

HUTCH'S PENNELL

Tying silk	black
Tail	golden pheasant tippet
Rib	fine oval silver tinsel
Body	bronze peacock herl tied thin
Hackles	black hen with a small white hen hackle in front

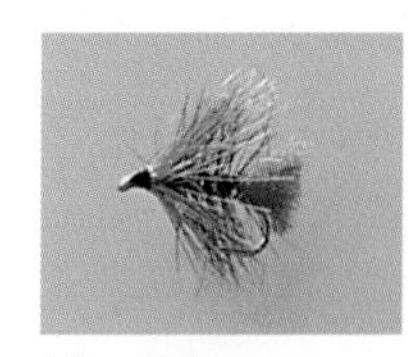

Blue Zulu

Black Ke-He

ORANGE KE-HE

Tying silk	black
Tail	red floss with a few fibres of golden pheasant tippet over
Body	bronze peacock herl
Hackle	orange hen

BLACK KE-HE

Tying silk	black
Tail	red floss with a few fibres of golden pheasant tippet over
Body	bronze peacock herl
Hackle	black hen

Oakham Orange

RED SPOT PALMER

Tying silk	brown
Rib	oval gold tinsel
Body	in three parts - peacock herl front and tail with red seals fur in the middle
Hackle	red game palmered

OAKHAM ORANGE

Tying silk	red
Tail	whiskers of hot orange cock hackle
Body	silver tinsel
Rib	oval silver tinsel
Body hackle	hot orange cock
Head hackle	two hot orange cock
Head	red varnish

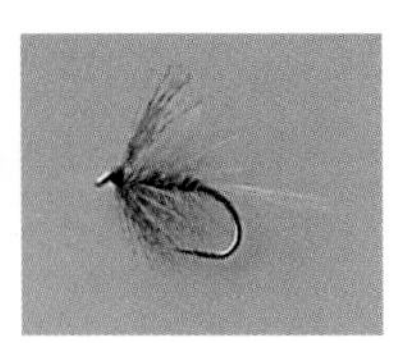

Kate Mclaren

KATE MCLAREN

Tying silk	black
Tail	golden pheasant topping
Rib	oval silver tinsel
Body	black seals fur
Body hackle	black cock
Head hackle	red game cock

POACHER

Tying silk	black
Tail	fibres of red golden pheasant body feather
Rib	oval gold tinsel
Body	rear third amber seals fur, front two thirds peacock herl
Hackle	furnace cock or hen

Golden Olive Bumble

GOLDEN OLIVE BUMBLE

Tying silk	brown
Tail	golden pheasant topping
Rib	oval gold tinsel
Body	golden-olive seals fur
Body hackle	golden olive and red game cock wound together
Head hackle	blue jay

CLARET BUMBLE

Tying silk	brown
Tail	golden pheasant tippet
Rib	oval gold tinsel
Body	claret seals fur
Body hackle	a black and claret cock wound together
Head hackle	blue jay

GENERAL SAFETY TIPS

Many angling locations are remote and certainly, if angling alone, it is advisable to inform someone where you are going in case of emergency. Some areas are subject to sudden weather changes, in particular the higher hill areas. It is advisable to carry a map and compass, and to wear warm clothing as a change from a clear day to thick mist can occur in minutes. When wading, few lochs can be considered totally safe especially if you are fishing alone and there are some which can be regarded as positively dangerous. Hidden underwater hazards include large rocks, holes and areas of soft mud which are not always made apparent by the surrounding terrain. In many lochs it is not necessary to wade as good fishing can be had close to the shore. Remember - IF IN DOUBT, DON'T WADE.

THE COUNTRY CODE

Access to many of the lochs is by obvious routes or tracks and anglers are asked to observe the country code by shutting gates, by not damaging walls or fences and by not leaving litter. Be considerate in parking, do not obstruct access roads and do not block passing places on single track roads; if you are not sure of access rights, ask. Do not unnecessarily annoy wildlife, especially nesting birds, which occupy most waterside locations and islands during the breeding season.

A basket from Clings Water Loch.

FISH SEASONS, SIZES AND LIMITS

FISH SPECIES	SEASON	SIZE LIMIT
BROWN TROUT:	15th March-6th October	10 inches
SEA TROUT:	25th February-31st October	12 inches
CHAR:	15th March-6th October	please return
SALMON:	25th February-31st October	

No basket limits are set by the SAA but anglers are requested to appreciate the need for conservation of stocks, especially sea trout. All undersized fish must be returned to the water.

THE LAW

Under Scottish Law it is illegal to:

1. fish for or take sea trout and salmon on a Sunday.
2. cast out tackle and leave it unattended, which constitutes a set line.
3. for a person to use more than one rod and line at any one time.

MAP REFERENCES AND KEY

In this book the numbers following the name of the loch are the sheet number of the Ordnance Survey Landranger series followed by the map reference. The individual loch maps are intended to give a general guide, some include hot spots IIIIII and all maps have north to the top.

There are few lochs south of Lerwick but one of the best known and popular lochs, Spiggie, lies a few miles north of the airport at the southern tip of Shetland. Most of the south mainland lochs are close to the road and are easily accessible.

SOUTH MAINLAND LOCHS

1 Loch of Spiggie

2 Loch of Clumlie

3 Loch of Vatsetter

4 Loch of Fladdabister

5 Loch of Brindister

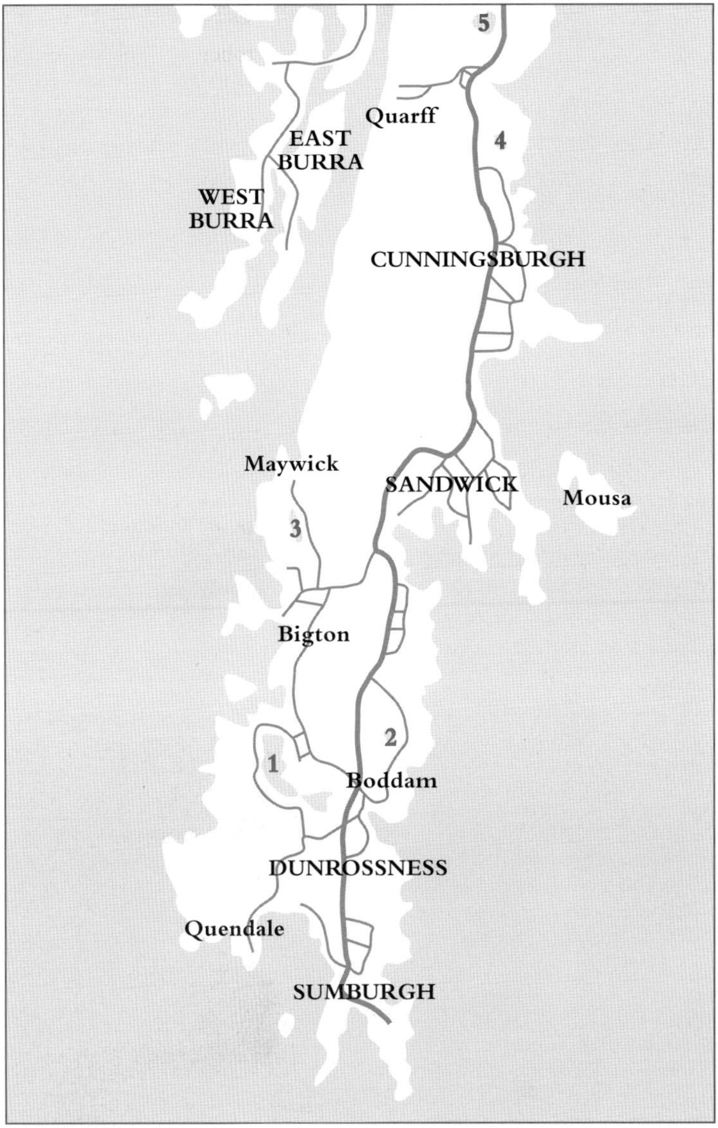

Loch of Spiggie
4/373166

/

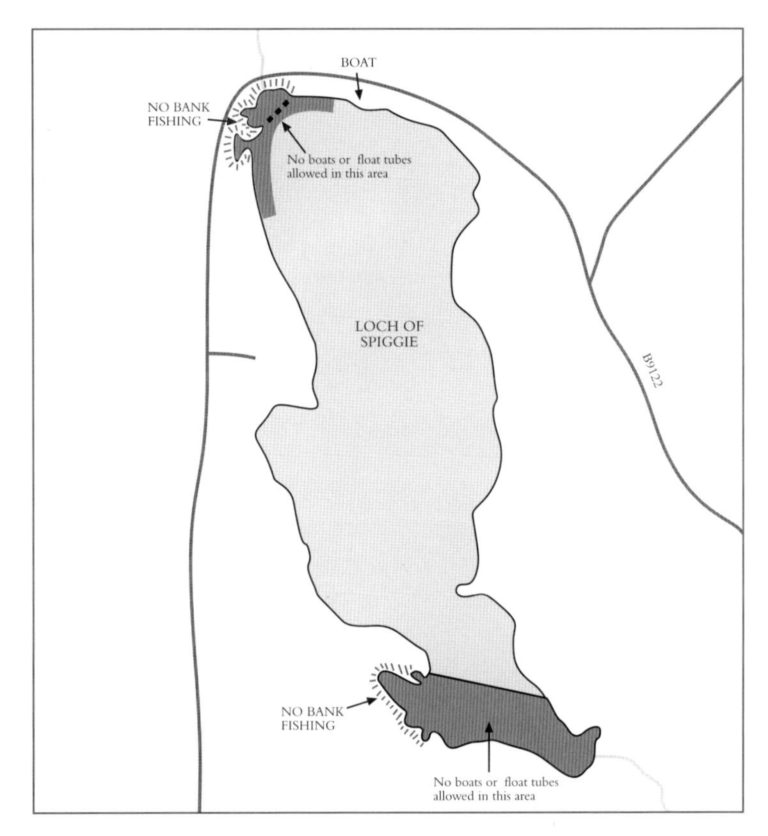

One of the largest lochs in Shetland and also a favourite of many local anglers. Owned by the RSPB and rented by the SAA there are a number of conditions imposed by the lease, details of which are supplied when you purchase your permit - these generally restrict the season, permit fly fishing only, control areas of angling and areas where boats may be used, and ban engines. The road passes the north and west shores and access may be had from a number of points along these shores. The boathouse and Association boat can be found at the north end.

Excellent for both bank and boat fishing and fish can be caught all over the loch. One of the favourite areas known as 'the deeps' is at the north end but a pair of chest waders is required to reach it. Wading is generally safe but beware of 'swan holes' in the sandy bottom at the north end. Good quality brown trout average about 10 ounces but there are fish to 3 pounds plus. Some sea trout from August.

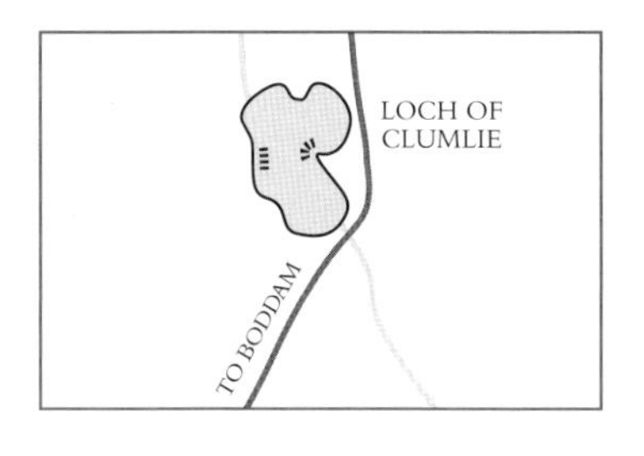

This small loch lies about a couple of miles east of Spiggie and is worth a few casts if you are in the area. Wading is not recommended as the bottom is a mixture of soft mud and slippery stones. Brown trout average 8 ounces with the occasional fish of a pound plus. Weeds up later in the season.

Loch of Clumlie

4/405175

2

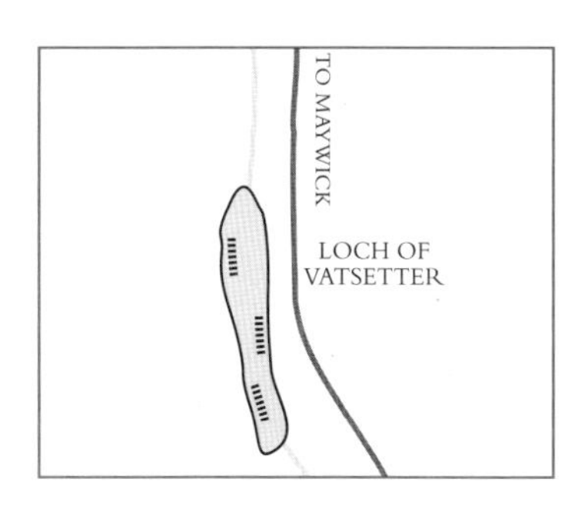

This long, narrow loch lies close to the road half a mile south of Maywick. Good-quality brown trout average 12 ounces with a few fish over the pound. No need to wade as there is deepish water close to shore. The north west corner is a favoured spot.

Loch of Vatsetter

4/379233

3

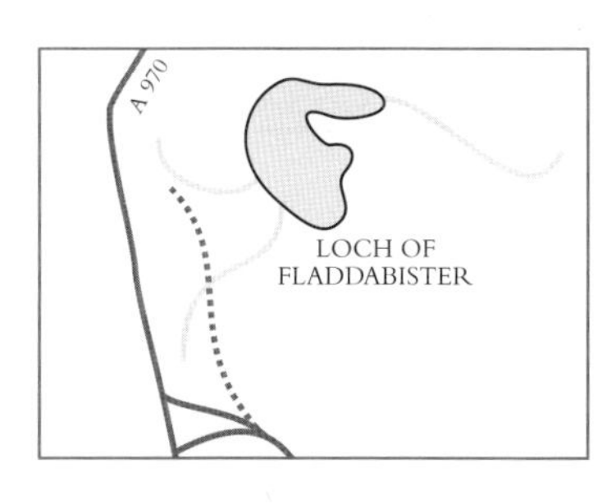

Lies about a mile south of Easter Quarff and is an easy ten minute walk east from the main Lerwick to Sumburgh road. Typical hill-loch trout which average about three to the pound. Some weed patches from mid-summer onwards. A good loch for the beginner.

Loch of Fladdabister

4/433337

4

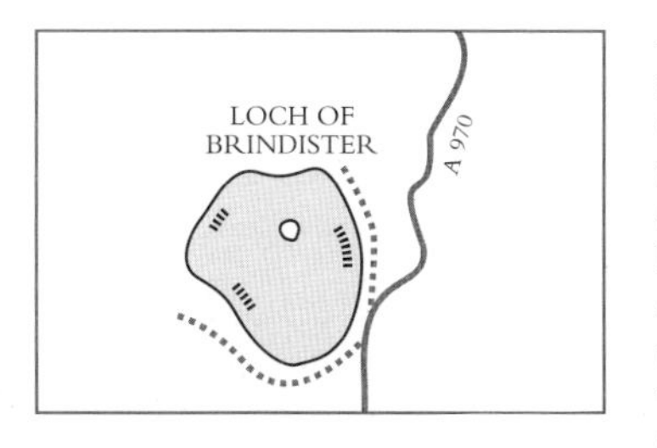

A water scheme loch close to the main road just north of Easter Quarff. Easy access via the peat track - shut all gates and do not obstruct the track. A clear water loch which fishes best in the evening. Good quality brown trout which average 12 ounces with some fish to 2 pounds plus. Generally safe wading. Occasionally stocked by the SAA.

Loch of Brindister

4/432370

5

LERWICK, SCALLOWAY & BRESSAY LOCHS

1 Trebister Loch
2 Sandy Loch
3 Gossa Water
4 Loch of Asta
5 Loch of Tingwall
6 Loch of Griesta
7 Broo Loch
Loch of Ustaness
Jamie Cheyne's Loch
Maggie Black's Loch
Loch of Garth
8 Loch of Strand
9 Loch of Setter
Loch of Brough
10 Beosetter Lochs
11 Loch of Grimsetter

There are a wide variety of lochs in this area, ranging from the heavily fished, clear water limestone lochs of the Tingwall Valley to the seldom fished group of hill lochs to the north of Scalloway. The often underrated Bressay lochs are recommended.

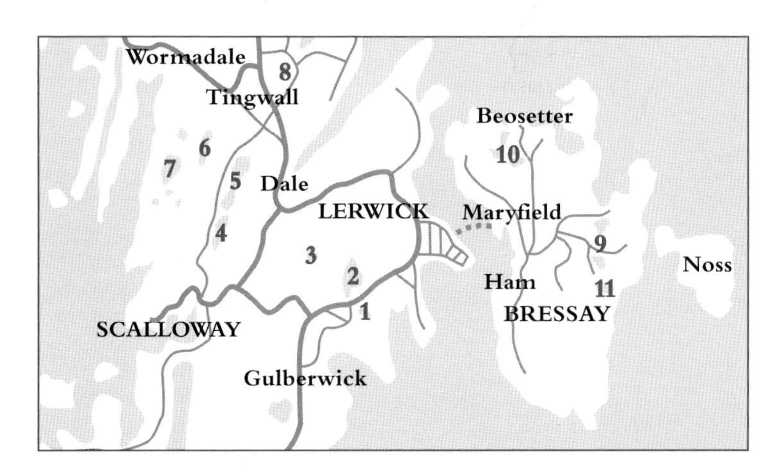

Trebister Loch

4/454395

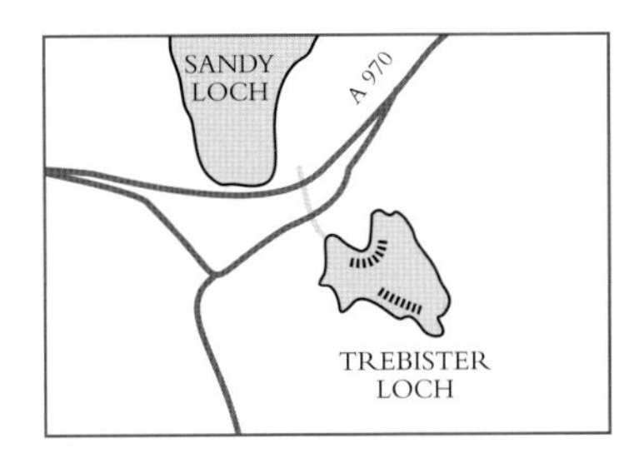

This small loch lies just south of Lerwick. Brown trout of 8 to 10 ounces but be ready for the occasional better fish. Wading is not recommended or neccessary as fish lie close in. All the standard loch patterns work well.

Sandy Loch

4/450405

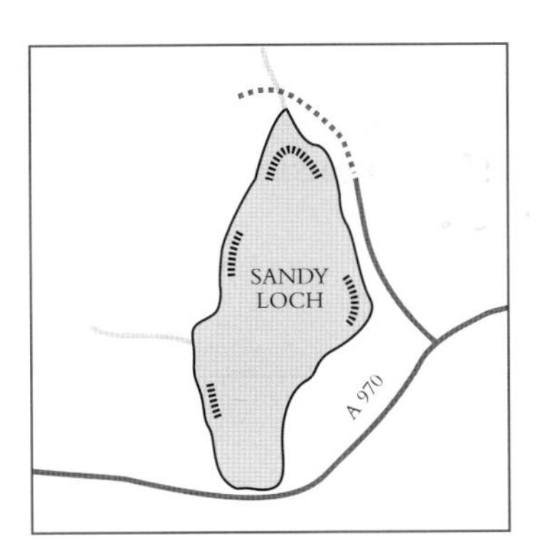

The public water supply for Lerwick. Easy access from the main road via the track which runs along the east and north sides of the loch. Very dark peaty water. Small dark-coloured brown trout which average three or four to the pound. Do not wade. A good loch for the beginner.

Gossa Water

4/439410

This small, shallow water is reached after a stiff 20 minute walk over the hill west of the Sandy Loch. Good quality brown trout. Wading is fairly safe and there are some weed patches from mid-summer onwards. The loch was stocked with fry in 1997.

Loch of Asta

4/413415

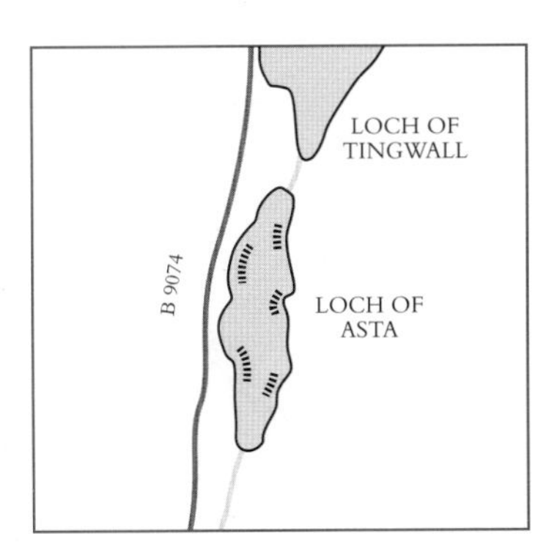

Easy access from the road. Do not obstruct gates or passing places. Good quality, silvery trout which average 8 ounces with an occasional fish over the pound. Lying on limestone the water is clear and of a high PH value. Generally safe wading and dark flies are said to work best. Good boat fishing.

Loch of Tingwall
4/415427

Takes it's name from the old norse 'lawting' or parliament which used to meet on the small, grassy point in the north west corner of the loch.
SAA are joint owners and have a boatshed, parking area and pier on the loch. One of the most popular lochs with local anglers. Strong fighting brown trout average 10 ounces with some fish over 2 pounds. The north part of the loch is coloured and shallow, the south is clearer and deeper - a depth of 85 feet has been recorded which is about 60 feet below sea-level.
The north end weeds up as the season progresses. Generally safe wading.
Stocked regularly by the SAA who have a boat for hire on the loch. Recommended.

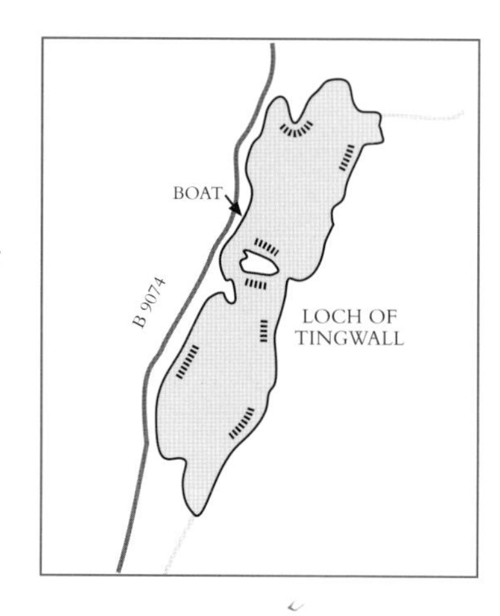

Loch of Griesta
4/409438

Access via the track from the north west end of Tingwall Loch up to the Griesta farm. Anglers must park at the farm and walk up the rough track to the lochside. Do not obstruct farm access. Good quality brown trout averaging 10 ounces with some fish to more than 2 pounds. Generally safe wading on the east side but there is deeper water on the west shore and wading is advised against. Some sea trout later in the season.

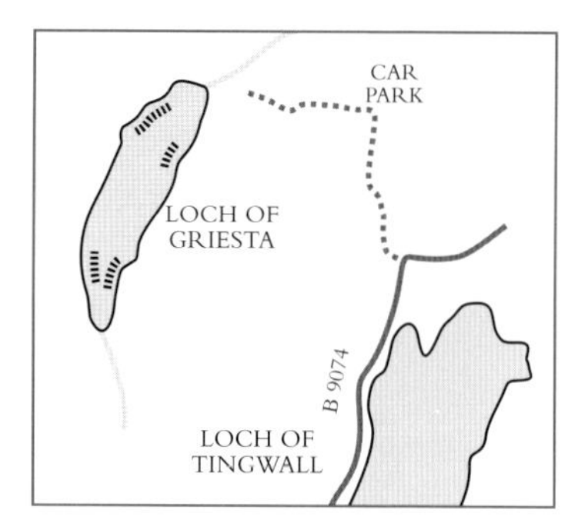

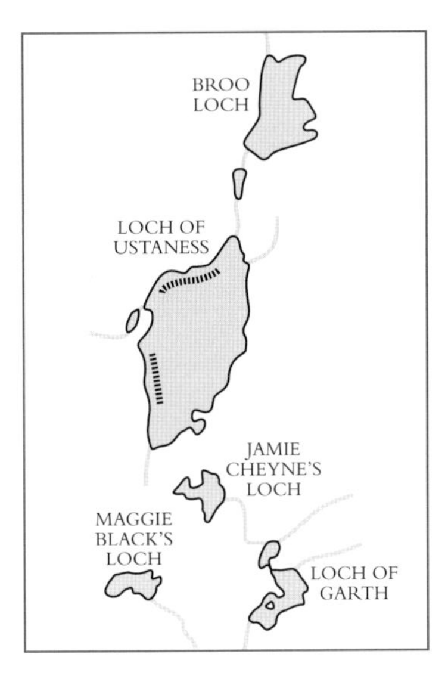

A group of lochs to the west and south of Griesta which require a bit of leg-work to reach.

Ustaness is the largest and deepest and the trout average 12 ounces. The west side is best for fly-fishing.

The trout in Broo and Garth are a couple of ounces smaller while Maggie Black's and Jamie Cheyne's are said to hold a few better-sized fish.

Broo Loch
4/402442

Loch of Ustaness
4/400432

Jamie Cheyne's Loch
4/400428

Maggie Black's Loch
4/397424

Loch of Garth
4/402423

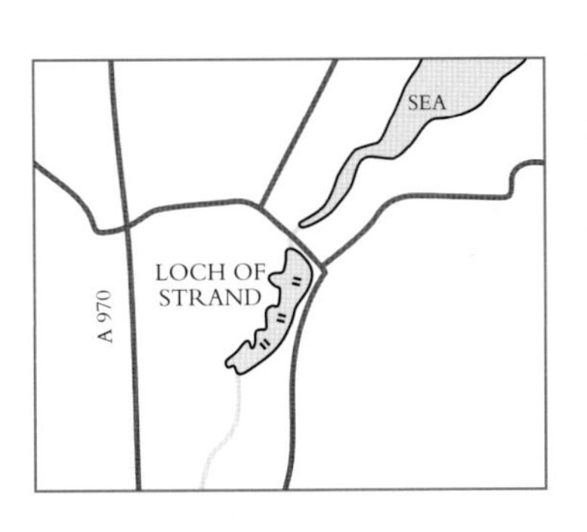

Well-known for it's sea trout fishing Strand is a small, brackish loch close to the sea. Access is easy from the old A970 road which runs along the side of the loch. The bottom of soft mud and slippery stones makes wading difficult. The sea trout enter the loch from mid-season onwards and there are also a few small brown trout.

Loch of Strand
4/431460

Loch of Setter
4/514418

A shallow loch which becomes weedy from mid-summer onwards. It holds trout which average about 10 ounces but there are a few fish to 2 pounds. Wade with care.

Loch of Brough
4/512408

This clear water loch is the local water supply and also holds some good fish though the average size is about 12 ounces. Can be dour but a good loch on it's day.

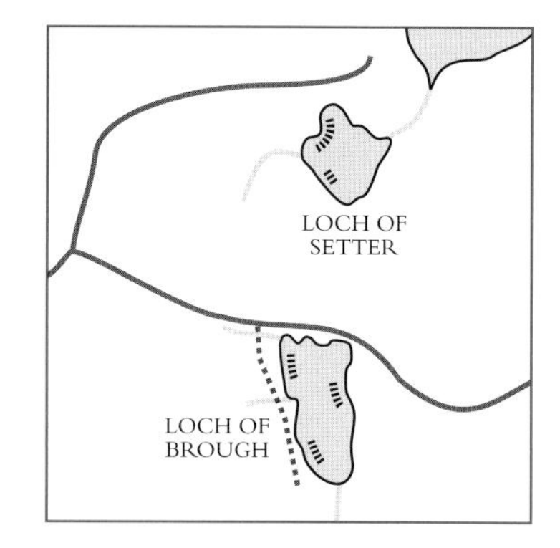

Beosetter Lochs
4/490437

A group of four lochs at the north end of the island all of which are ideal fly-fishing waters. The northmost (Mill Loch) holds trout which average about 12 ounces but fish of more than 2 pounds have been caught here. Weeds up in the summer and avoid wading at the south end where the bottom is soft mud.

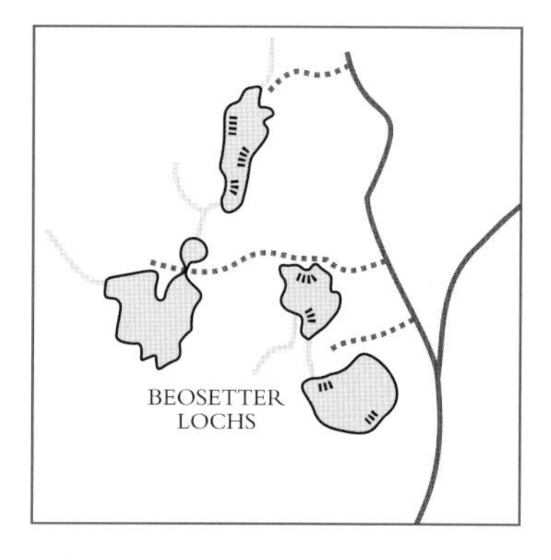

The western loch (Loch of Cruester) is a dour loch where fish of 4 pounds have been caught in the past. The fish in the two east lochs (Gunnista Lochs) average 12 ounces and there are fish of more than 2 pounds in both lochs. These lochs were stocked with fry in 1997. Wading is reasonably safe.

Loch of Grimsetter
4/520399

Follow the track which leaves the tarred road at the Loch of Brough and heads southwards. After about a mile you will see the loch down on your left below the house at Gorie. A shallow loch with a sandy bottom in places. The loch was stocked with fry in 1995 and 1996 for the first time by the Association and the loch will be watched with interest to see how well these fish grow.

CENTRAL MAINLAND LOCHS

The lochs in this area provide a good selection of easy access roadside lochs such as Girlsta, Sand Water and Petta Water, all of which hold good quality trout. For the more active, the remote hill lochs listed have the potential to provide a memorable day's fishing. The Loch of Voe, with its many trout, offers the chance for beginners to become "hooked" on fishing.

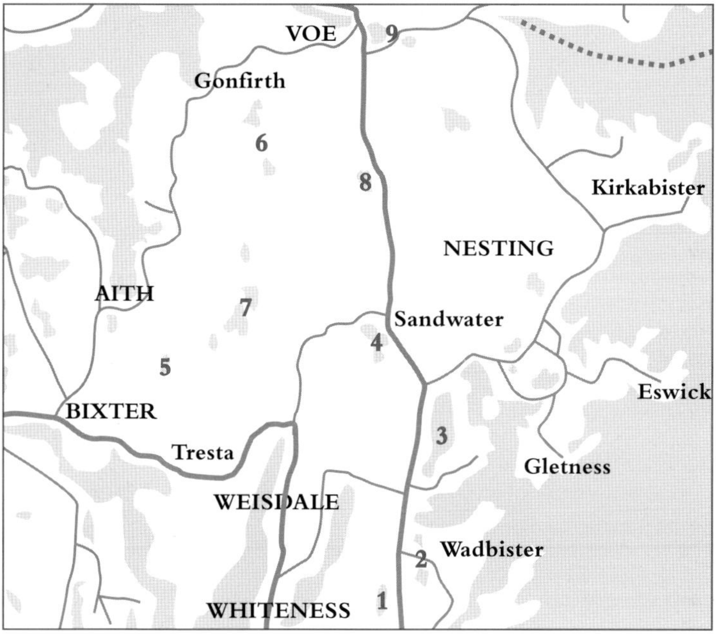

NORTH MAINLAND MAP

1 Longa Water

2 Black Loch
Loch of Vatster

3 Loch of Girlsta

4 Sand Water

5 Whitelaw Loch

6 Smerla Water
Marrowfield Water

7 Loch of Lunklet
Lamba Water
Maa Water
Truggles Water

8 Petta Water

9 Loch of Voe
Sae Water

Longa Water
3/419477

18

A deep, dour water little fished by local anglers. Reputed to hold good fish and spinning would probably be more effective than fly fishing.

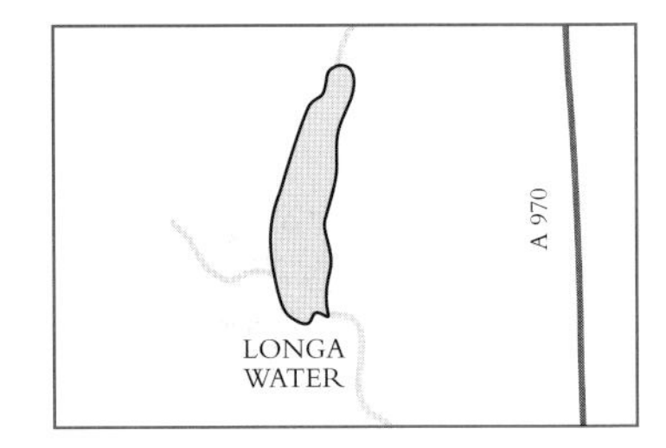

Black Loch
3/428492

Loch of Vatster
3/430483

19

Both lochs were popular in the past, before the decline in the numbers of sea trout running into them, but are now mostly ignored by local anglers. The brown trout are still there and they average about 8 ounces.

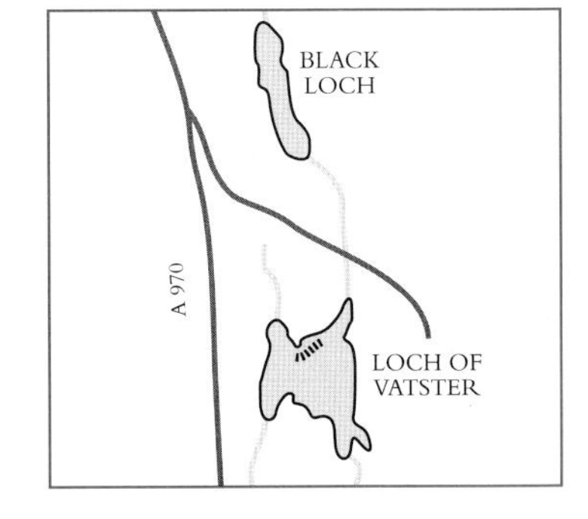

Loch of Girlsta
3/43352

20

The modern name comes from the old norse 'Geirhildarvatn'. Geirhild was a woman, who in saga times, was said to have drowned in the loch. The deepest and one of the largest of Shetland's lochs and also the only one to hold arctic char. A number of large brown trout have come from this water over the years - the heaviest recorded was over 12 pounds - but the average fish is about 10 ounces. The east shore is said to fish best. There is a parking area with boat access to the loch at the south end of the loch.

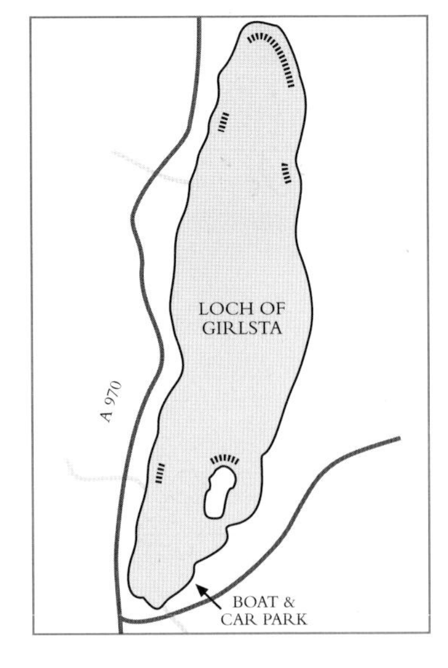

Sand Water
3/415545

21

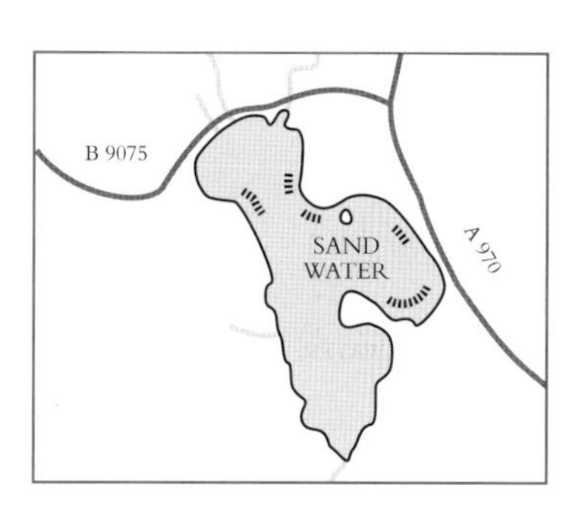

More popular in the past when the loch saw good runs of sea trout but is now fished mainly for it's brown trout. A shallow loch which can become coloured and unfishable in high winds. Easy wading and fish can be caught all over the loch. Brown trout average 8 ounces and the loch becomes weedy after mid-summer.

Whitelaw Loch
3/359540

22

A shallow, clear water loch which can grow large trout but needs regular stocking. It has been stocked on a number of occasions by the Association and in 1964 was stocked experimentally with rainbow trout but these soon died out. Stocked with fry in 1998 there should be takeable fish in 2000. Easiest way to approach the loch is via the track which leaves the B9071 at the Aith cemetery and heads southwards. Park at the pumphouse at the end of the track and the loch is a ten minute walk to the south east.

Smerla Water
3/382610

23

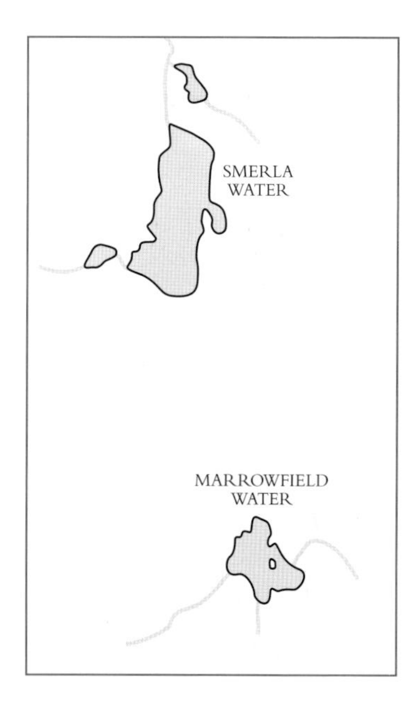

Park beside the Loch of Gonfirth on the B971 a couple of miles west of the village of Voe. A ten minute walk up the valley to the south will bring you to Smerla Water. The loch has a few shallower areas at the southern end where wading is possible but much of the loch has a rocky shore with deep water close to shore. Native hill-loch trout which are generally 8 ounces or less.

Marrowfield Water
3/387592

24

Marrowfield Water is a further 15 minute walk over the hill to the south and the fish are of a 6 to 8 ounce average but there are a few larger specimens in the loch also. There is a peaty bottom in places and there are few areas which could be waded safely.

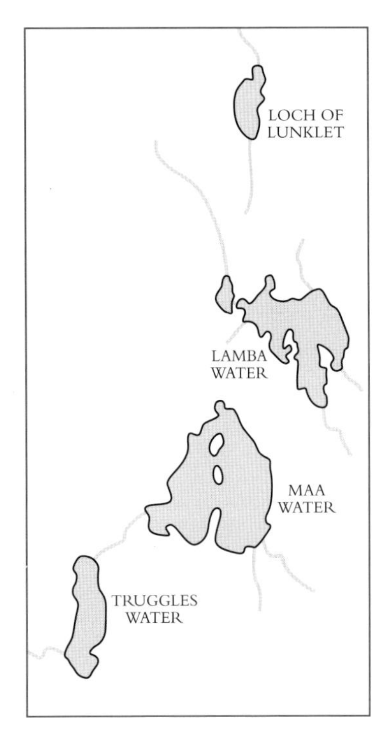

Loch of Lunklet
3/380570

Probably the easiest way to these lochs is to follow the burn up to the Loch of Lunklet. Park at the bridge at the head of East Burra Firth and follow the path beside the burn. Where the burn forks follow the path left and the Loch of Lunklet is a further 15 minutes walk. The Loch of Lunklet is small and shallow and weeds up in places later in the season. There are plenty of hard-fighting little trout of 4 to 8 ounces in the loch and good numbers can be caught.

Lamba Water
3/382560

Lamba Water trout average about 10 ounces and four to six fish would be a normal basket. There is no need to wade as there is deep water close to shore and the fish lie close in.

Maa Water
3/378552

Maa Water also has deep water close to shore, especially at the north end, but the loch is shallower towards the south end. Again the trout are about 8 to 10 ounces but there are some better fish of a pound or more.

Truggles Water
3/371546

Truggles Water completes the quartet and this is a shallow water especially on the west side of the loch. There are good numbers of 6 to 8 ounce fish and the east side seems to be most productive.

Petta Water

3/417590

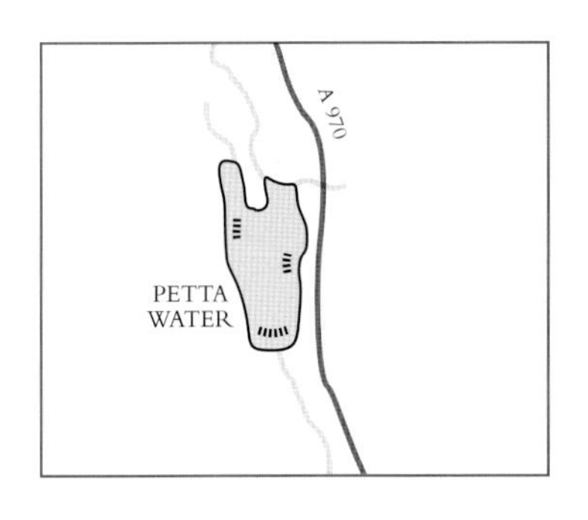

Petta is derived from the old norse 'Pettr' which was the Viking's name for the pictish people who inhabited Shetland in the past. This is a fairly shallow loch which is best fished early in the season before the weed becomes too thick. Wading is mostly safe but beware of a few soft areas on the road side. The trout average about 10 ounces with the occasional fish up to 2 pounds.

Loch of Voe

3/417627

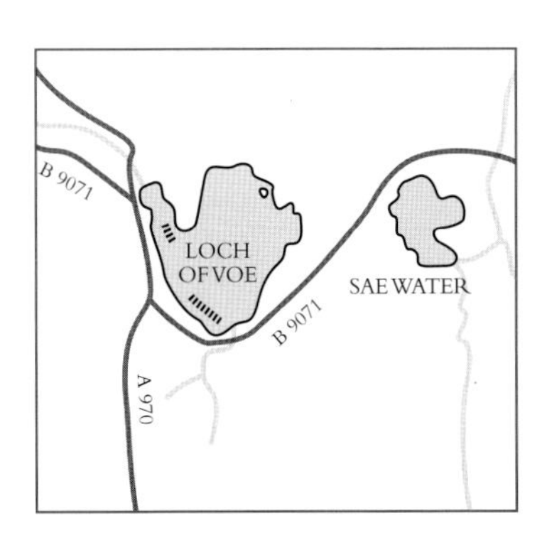

A good loch for the beginner with plenty of small fish and baskets of 20 and more are possible. Wading is safe from the shingle beach at the south end but slippery stones on the other shores makes wading unwise.

Sae Water

3/422629

Small and shallow, this loch was fished in the past for the sea trout which entered the loch via the Laxo Burn. A few small fish may still enter the loch but it is rarely fished now. Very weedy, especially along the west side, and the brown trout are mostly small.

WEST MAINLAND LOCHS

This area has dozens of lochs where the visiting angler can find good fishing. There are a number of good lochs close to the road to suit the less active angler and for the walker/angler there are many lochs among the hills where peace and solitude is guaranteed.

1 Loch of Northouse

2 Loch of Vaara

3 Loch of Aithsness

4 Loch of Clousta

5 Loch of Hostigates

6 Turdale Water

7 Kirkhouse Water, Loch of Collaster

8 Clings Water

9 Hulma Water

10 Sand Water, Forse Water

11 Grass Water, Culeryn

12 Mill Loch, Quassawall Loch

13 Heillia Water

14 Smalla Waters

15 Loch of Hollorin

16 Sulma Water

17 Longa Water, Djuba Water, Houlma Water

18 Mousa Water

19 Loch of Brunatwatt

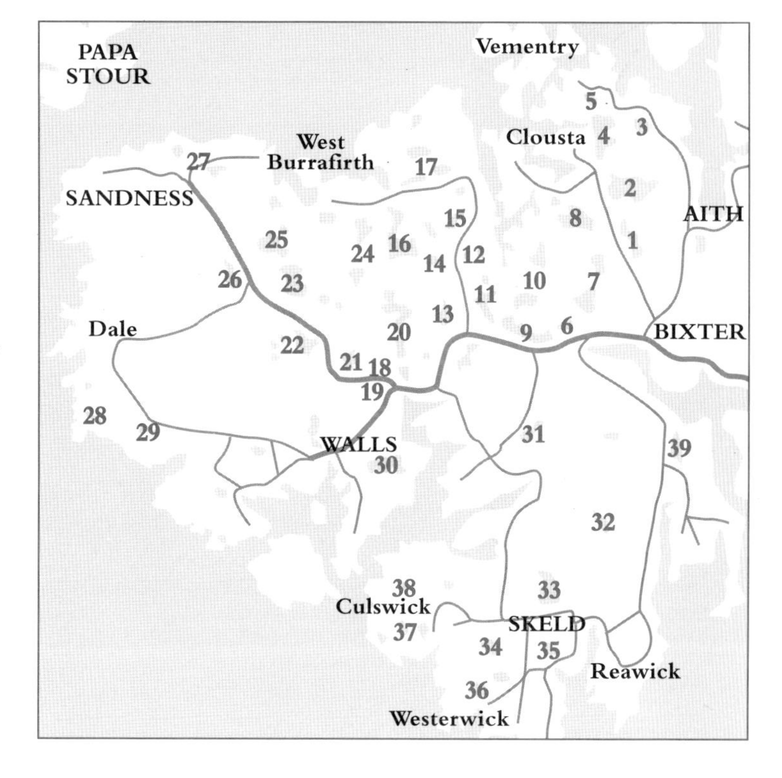

20 Loch of Brouster, Loch of Voxterby

21 Loch of Flatpunds

22 Lunga Water, Sma' Lochs

23 Burga Water

24 Galta Water, Daney's Loch

25 Mousavord Loch, Djuba Water

26 Stanevatstoe Loch

27 Loch of Collaster, Loch of Norby

28 Loch of Watsness

29 Loch of Sung

30 Loch of Grunnavoe

31 Loch of Gruting

32 Sand Water

33 Gossa Water

34 Housa Water

35 Loch of Arg

36 Loch of Westerwick

37 Sand Water, Loch of Sotersta, Loch of Broch

38 Vivilie Loch

39 Loch of Semblister

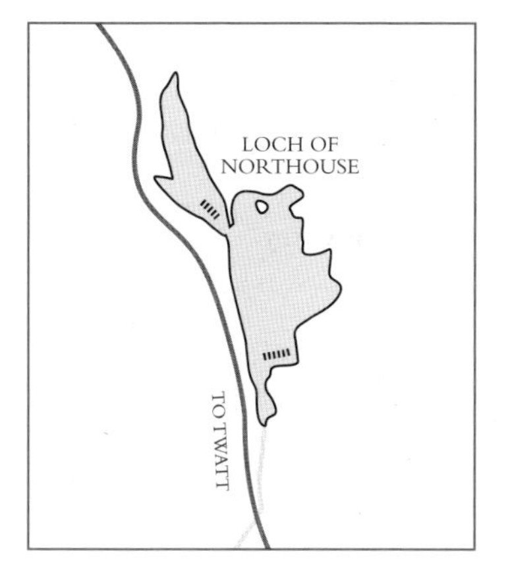

Loch of Northouse
3/325550

A loch of two halves - the southern part being the largest and deepest. Both parts are mostly weed-free and wading is generally safe. Top-quality, hard fighting brown trout which average 12 ounces but both lochs contain fish of more than 3 pounds. Algal blooms can occur.

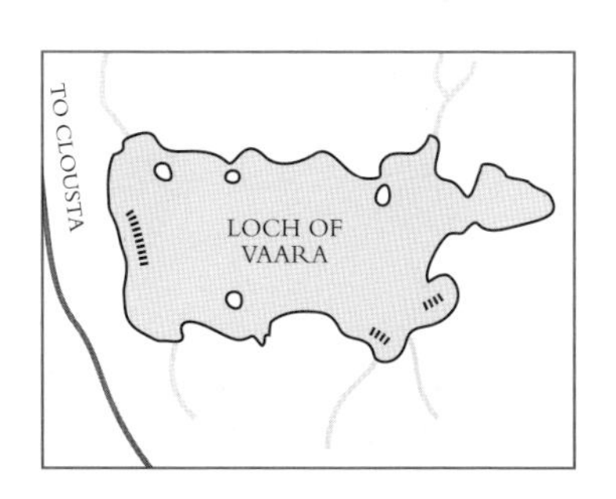

Loch of Vaara
3/325568

A large, deep loch which in the past had a reputation for baskets of mainly small fish but an improvement in size has been seen in recent years and the occasional fish over the pound is not unusual. Dangerous wading in some areas.

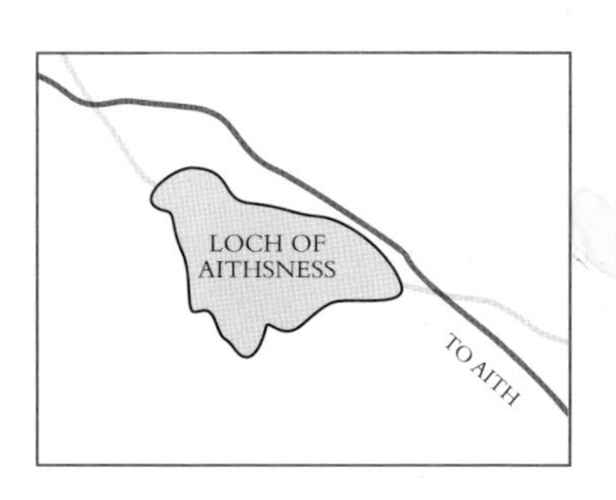

Loch of Aithsness
3/330584

This is a deep loch with mostly small fish which average about 6 ounces. Some weed close to the north west shore later in the season.

Loch of Clousta
3/317580

A large, shallowish loch with many fishy bays and islands. There is easy access to the north end of the loch from the Aith to Vementry road and to fish the south end you can park at the end of the Bixter to Clousta road. Beware of holes in the heather-covered hillsides around the north end. The brown trout average about 8 ounces and fish can be caught all round the loch. In the past good runs of sea trout entered the loch but catches have now declined greatly. A good loch for boat fishing but beware of rocks just below the surface. The Association has a boat here which is kept at the south end below the manse.

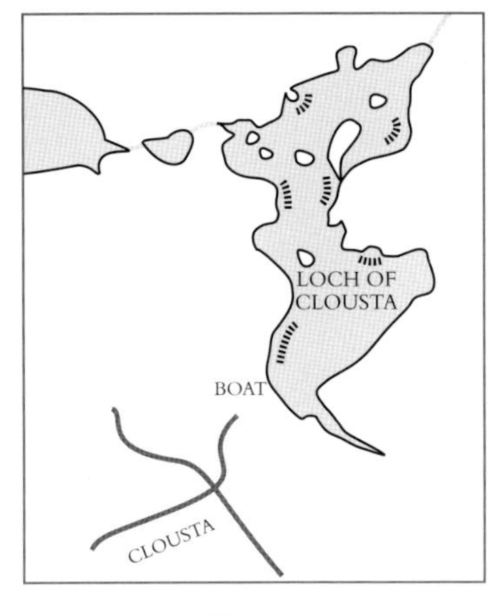

29 BOAT

Loch of Hostigates
3/312592

A small but deep loch which holds top quality, hard fighting trout up to 2 pounds though the average size is less than a pound. Deep water close to shore so no need to wade. The far side from the road is the place to start.

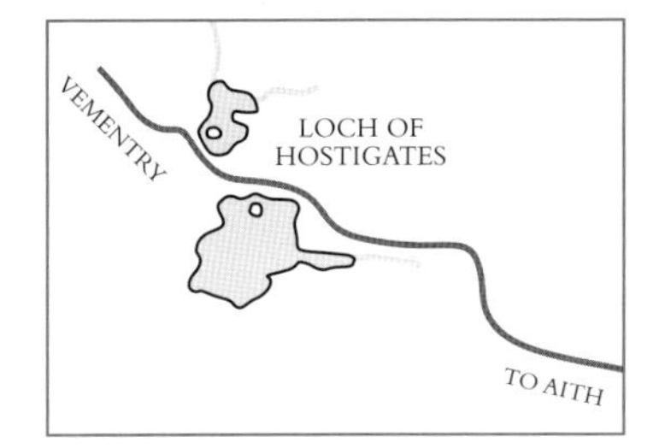

Turdale Water
3/307530

A short track which leaves the main road just west of Park Hall will take you to the east shore of the loch (shut all gates). This small, shallow water can produce fish of more than 2 pounds but the average size is about 10 ounces. Wading is safe in most areas. Can be affected by algal bloom in hot weather.

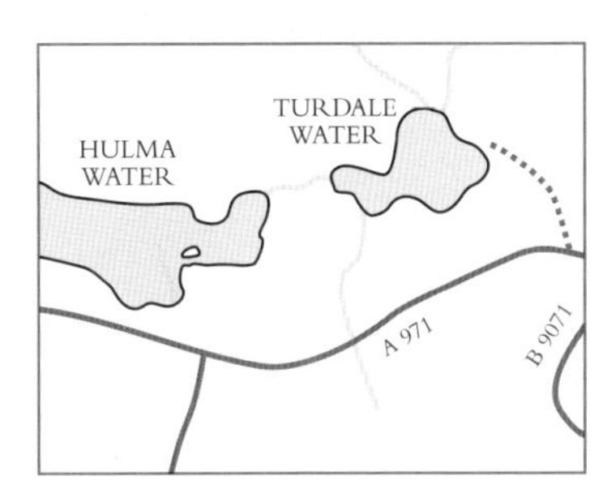

Kirkhouse Water
3/311537

Loch of Collaster
3/316546

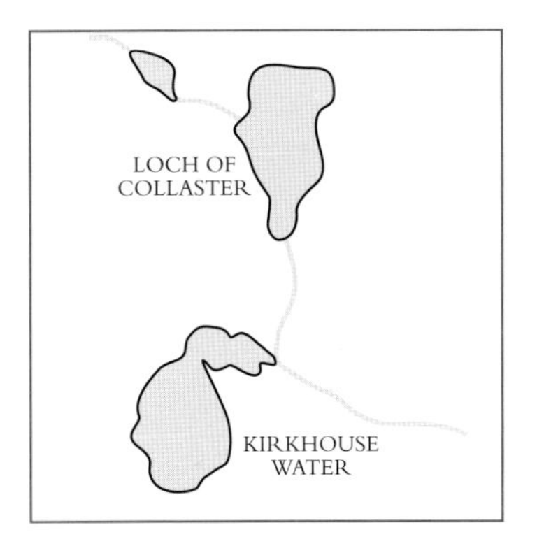

Both lochs hold hard-fighting silvery fish which average about 12 ounces but fish of more than 2 pounds have been caught. Deepest water on the west side of the lochs and care should be taken when wading.

Clings Water
3/310560

30

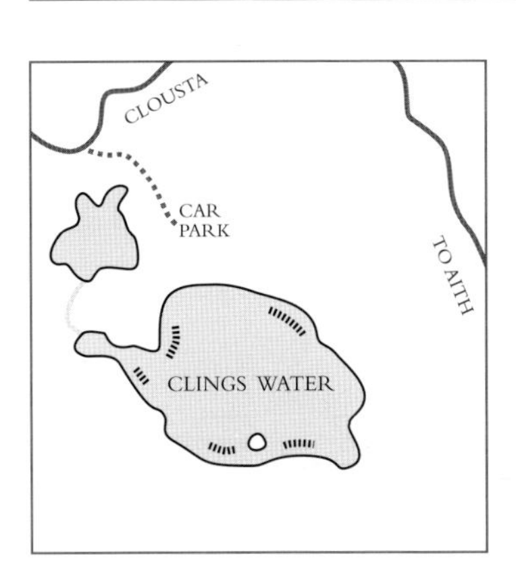

Take a left at the junction near the end of the Clousta road and after about half a mile take the farm track on your left. Stocked with Loch Leven trout many years ago this is a popular loch with many local anglers. Good quality brown trout which average about 12 ounces with some fish to more than 2 pounds.

Hulma Water
3/295529

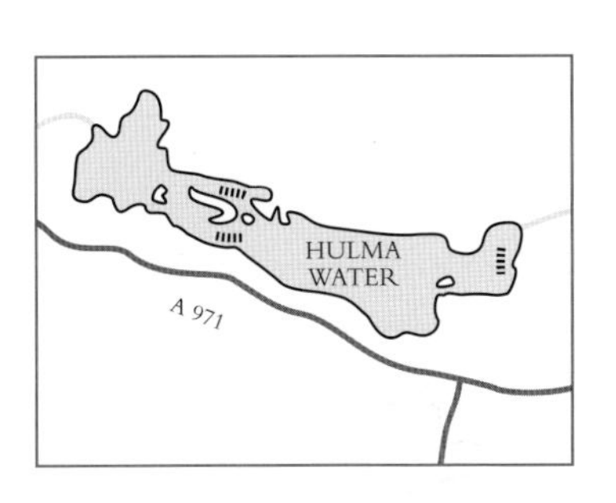

This long, narrow loch lies close to the A971 just a mile beyond Turdale Water. An average basket would be three or four fish weighing a couple of pounds. The best areas seem to be among the islands and the shallow bay at the east end. Some weed patches at the north end of the loch. Good boat fishing.

Sand Water
3/297548

A ten minute walk north west-wards from the west end of Hulma Water brings you to this deeper water with typical hill-loch brownies of 6 to 8 ounces.

Forse Water
3/300550

This loch is a further 15 minute walk north from Sand Water and holds a good stock of 6 to 12 ounce fish. Free-rising trout in peaceful surroundings.

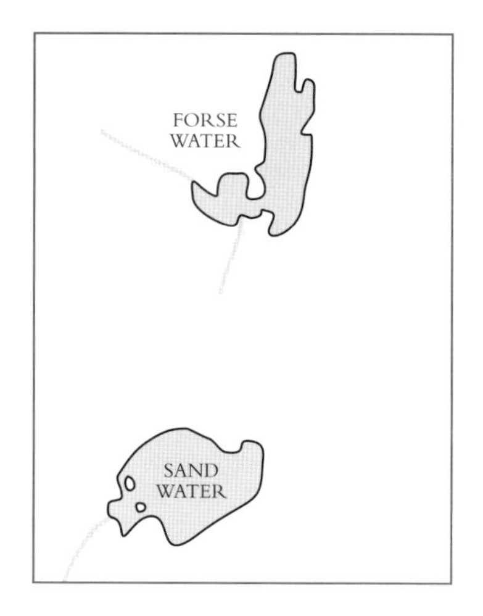

Grass Water
3/285535

In the past these two lochs saw a run of sea trout but are now fished mostly for their brown trout which are plentiful and mostly small.

Culeryin
3/286542

Culeryin becomes very weedy and the trout average about four to the pound. Grass Water trout average twice that size and are caught all over the loch. Wading is not neccessary as fish lie close to the shore.

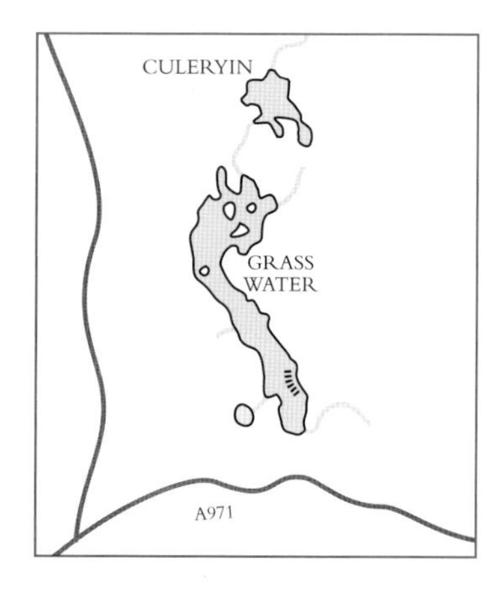

Mill Loch
3/282550

Quassawall Loch
3/279550

These two lochs lie close to the West Burrafirth road at Newton. The Mill Loch contains mostly small fish whilst Quassawall Loch holds a better class of fish averaging 8 to 10 ounces with some fish over the pound. The latter becomes weedy as the season progresses.

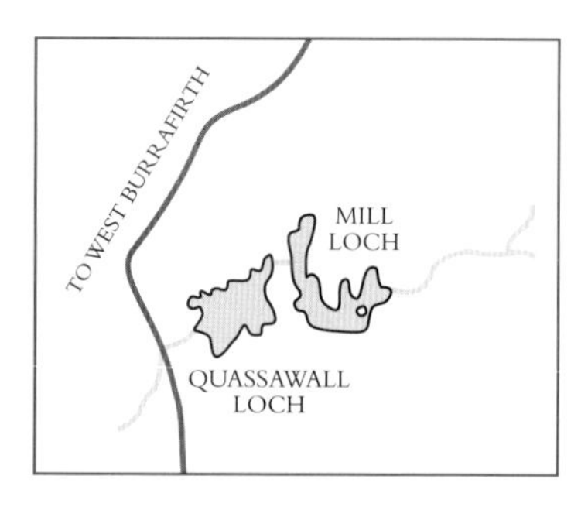

Heillia Water

3/273532

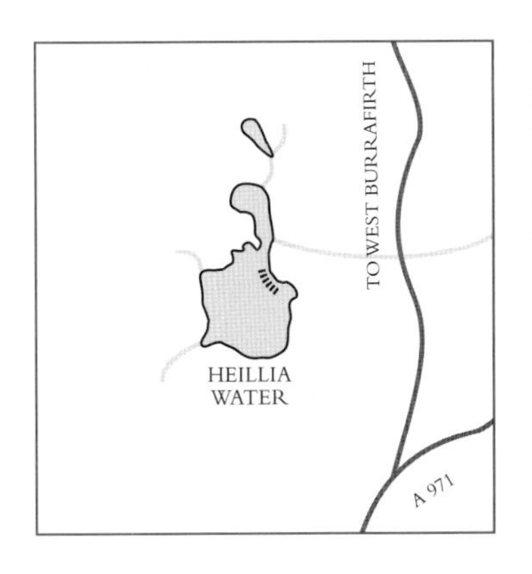

The north part seems to hold a good stock of small fish of the 6 ounce size while the deeper south section holds fish averaging 10 ounces with the occasional fish over a pound.

Smalla Waters

3/270548

A group of four lochs but only two are worth fishing - the largest and the one to the north of it. The larger loch has deep water close to shore and the other is shallower and more weedy. The trout in both average 10 ounces but be prepared because there are some better fish.

Loch of Hollorin

3/275558

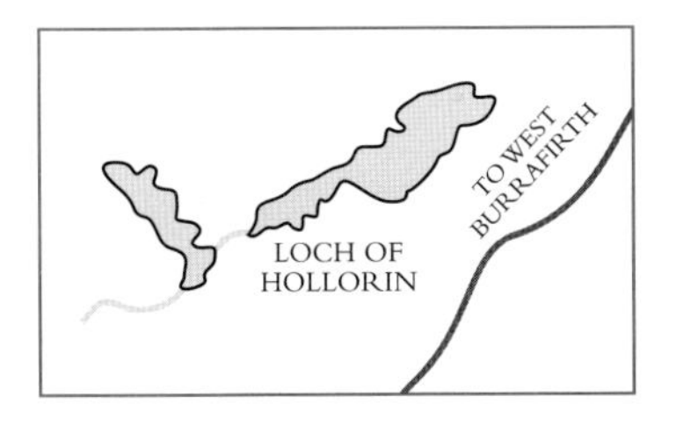

Park in the small quarry beside the road above Newton and a short walk to the north west will bring you to the loch. The water is crystal clear and the trout are bright, silvery fish with a good average weight of just under a pound with some fish of over 2 pounds. Can be dour at times and weeds up in the late season. Stocked with fry in 1998.

Sulma Water
3/260555

Just to the north west of the Smalla Waters this much larger loch has a wealth of fishy bays and points with a couple of islands thrown in. Most of the favourite spots seem to be in the south end but fish can be caught anywhere. Fish lie close to the shore and wading is not required. Well-suited for boat fishing.

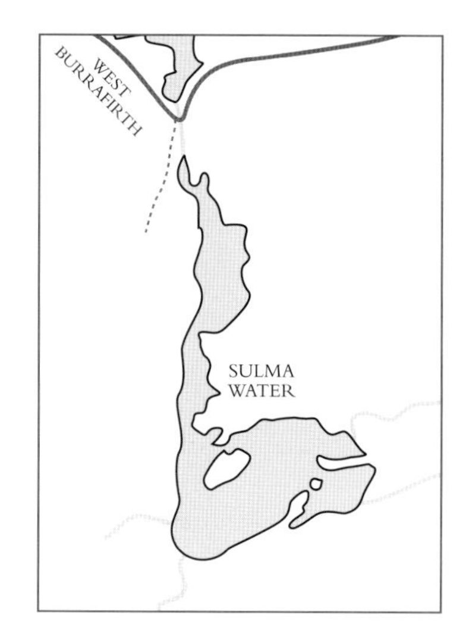

Longa Water
3/265570

Djuba Water
3/275573

Houlma Water
3/266576

Lunga Water is nearest the road and contains traditional hill-loch trout of about 8 ounces. No need to wade as fish lie close to shore. Djuba Water is a clear-water loch which can be dour at times but it holds some better fish between 1 and 2 pounds. Houlma Water also has some decent fish which can reach 2 pounds. Again wading is unneccessary. Please be considerate about parking and do not obstruct the access of vehicles to "Modesty" croft.

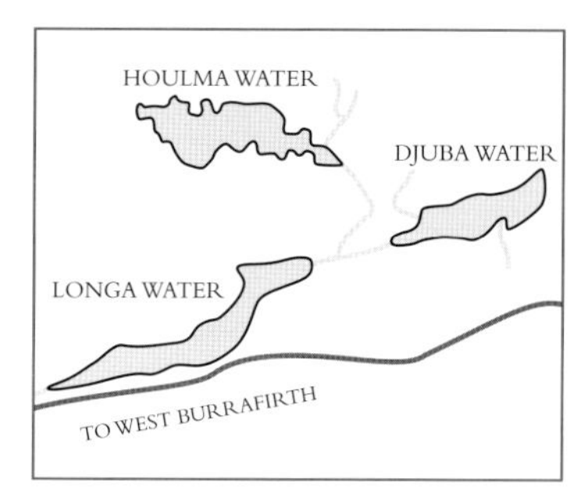

Mousa Water
3/251518

A small, dour water which is little fished though there are reports of some decent fish caught in the past.

Loch of Brunatwatt
3/251511

Shallow and weedy this loch holds a good stock of bright little fish which average three or four to the pound.

Loch of Brouster
3/260520

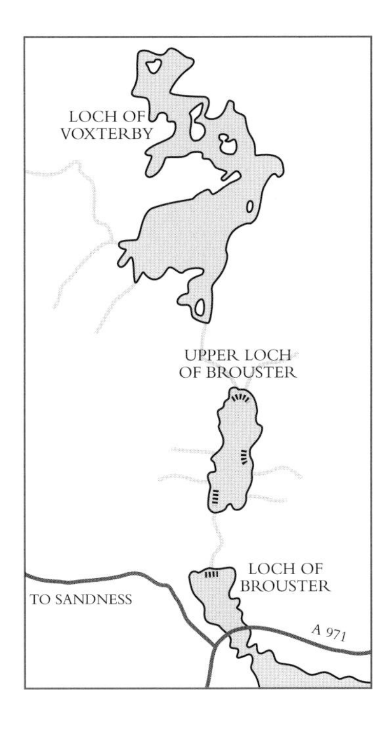

Park at the Bridge of Walls where there is a tidal pool behind the bridge. This was one of Shetland's premier sea trout fisheries and there is still a decent run of fish into these two lochs in the autumn. From the north end of the tidal pool a short walk up the burn will take you to Upper Loch of Brouster which holds typical hill-loch brownies of 6 to 8 ounces. Deeper water on the east side and a rocky shore makes wading unwise.

Loch of Voxterby
3/260535

The much larger Loch of Voxterby is a further ten minute walk north from Brouster. This is a water of many small bays and islands where you are unlikely to be disturbed. The north half of the loch seems to fish best and a good day should result in a basket of about a dozen fish for 5 or 6 pounds.

Loch of Flatpunds
3/247520

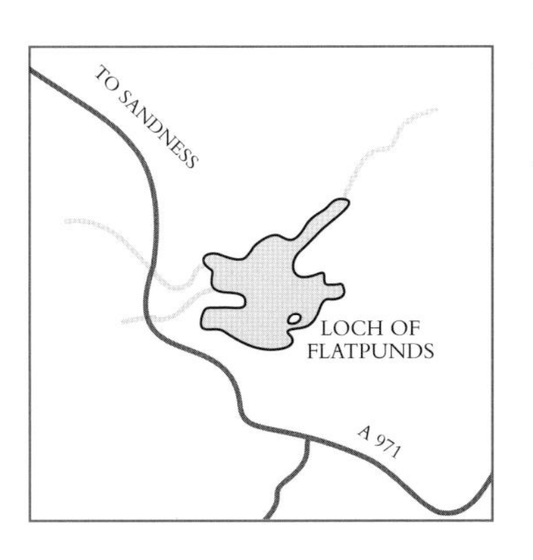

A dark, rocky loch with small, dark coloured trout which average about 8 ounces. Take care if wading.

Lunga Water
3/235527

Lunga Water lies close to the A971 and is the water supply for the area. With deep water close to the shore wading is not really neccessary. Expect native hill-loch trout of about 8 ounces with an occasional fish over a pound.

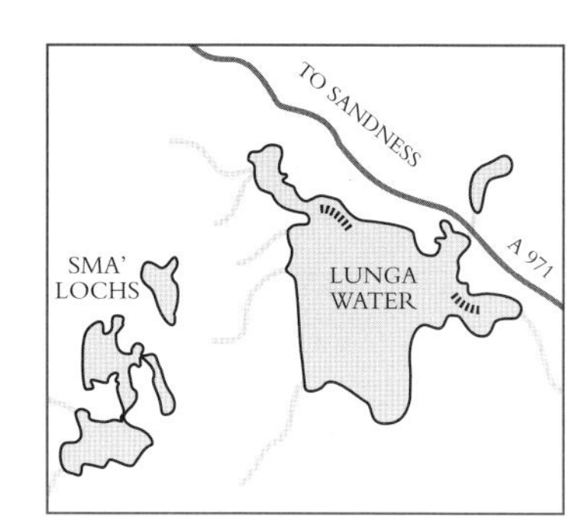

Sma' Lochs
3/227522

The two Sma' Lochs are a ten minute walk over the hill from the west side of Lunga Water. Both are small and shallow and the trout average about 10 ounces. The northmost loch holds some silvery trout as well as the normal darker coloured brown trout.

Burga Water
3/232540

This large loch lies in a hollow a short walk from the road. Fish can be caught all over the loch and average 6 to 8 ounces. The ruins of an iron age dun or fort can be seen on the small island in the south east corner of the loch. There are two small lochs to the south east which hold good numbers of 6 ounce fish.

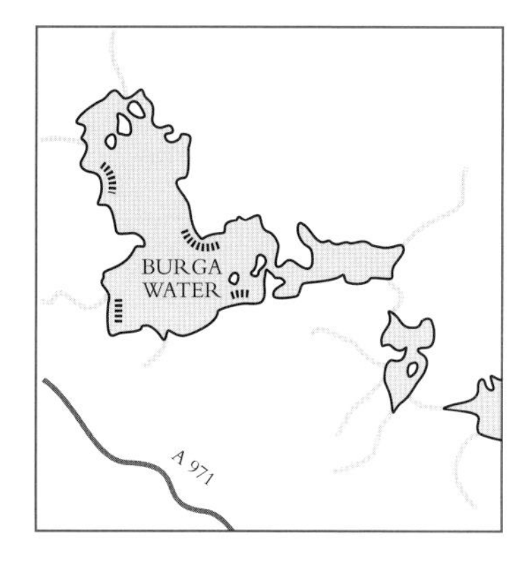

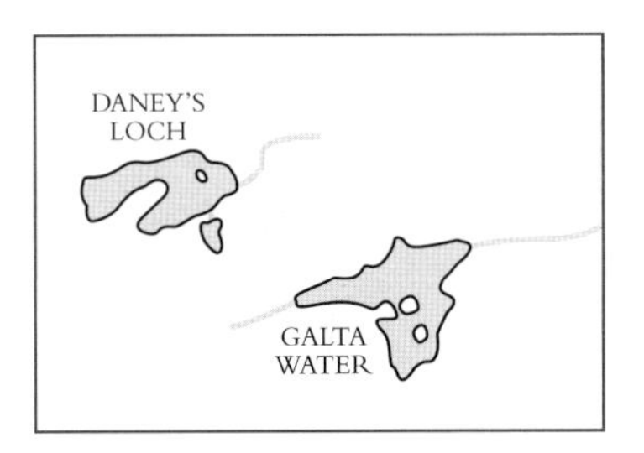

Galta Water
3/248542

Further into the hills east of Burga Water these lochs are situated among some of the best hill-walking country in Shetland.

Galta Water can produce fish of more than a pound but most are between 6 and 10 ounces.

Daney's Loch
3/240548

Daney's loch is deeper and more dour and is said to hold some good fish but they are not easy to catch.

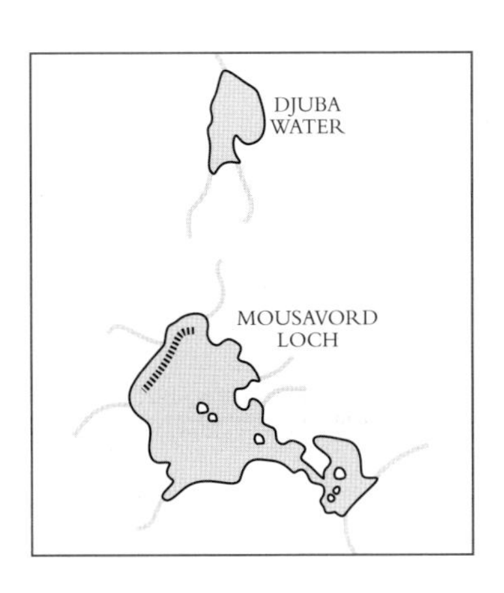

Mousavord Loch
3/224553

Mousavord is the largest and holds good numbers of typical hill-loch trout of 6 to 8 ounce. There is deep water close to the shore for much of the shoreline.

Djuba Water
3/226562

Djuba Water holds fish of better quality with an average of 12 ounces.

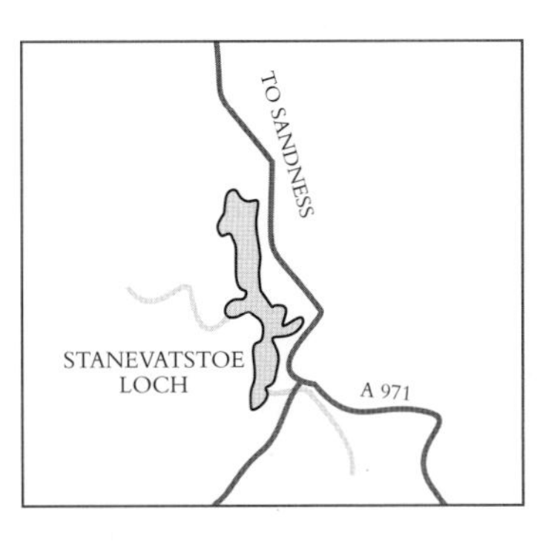

Stanevatstoe Loch
3/217543

A weedy roadside loch which holds mostly small trout.

Loch of Collaster
3/210572

Loch of Norby
3/200578

Both lochs produce bright, fat little trout most of which are less than 8 ounces. Quite a lot of weed in both lochs from mid-summer.

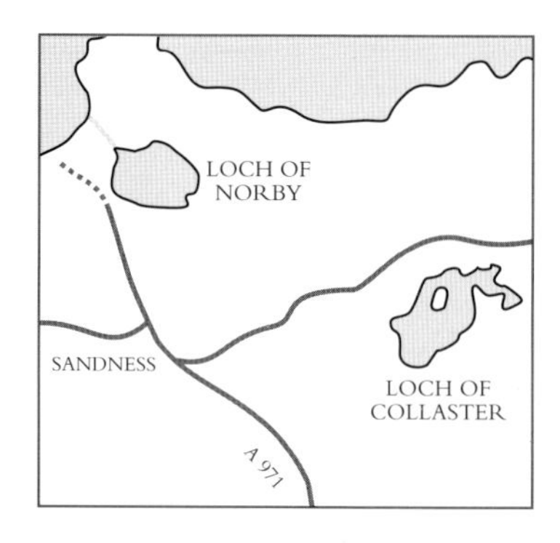

Loch of Watsness
3/175505

In the past this loch was said to be fishless but the association stocked it in 1996. This is a fertile, clear water loch which should provide plenty of feed and the fish should grow well.

Loch of Sung
3/192501

This small, shallow water is a short walk from the road and holds mainly small hill-loch trout.

Loch of Grunnavoe
3/260490

Lying close to the village of Walls this largish loch normally gives up fish of 6 to 8 ounces but occasionally a few better fish show up. The south shore is probably best and the loch would suit boat fishing very well.

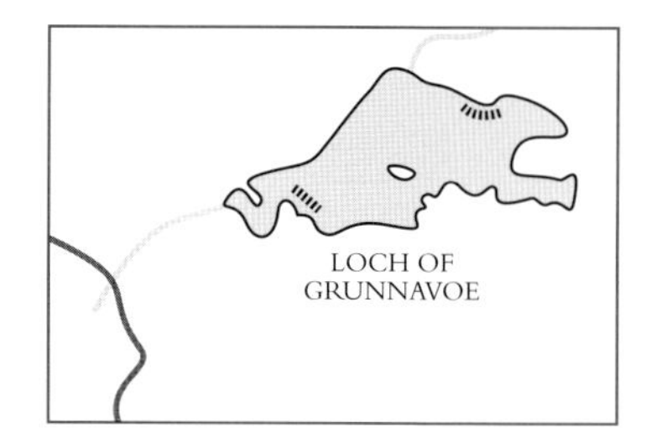

Loch of Gruting
3/295502

This small, shallow loch becomes very weedy as the season progresses and the brown trout are mostly small. In the past it was fished for the run of sea trout which came up the burn from ScuttaVoe but is now seldom fished.

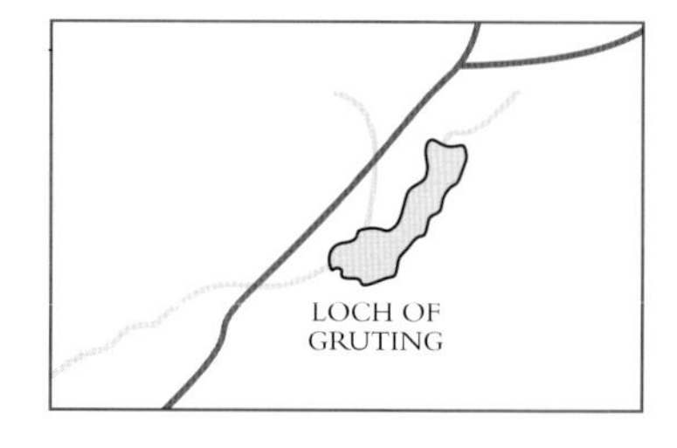

Sand Water
3/317478

A typical hill-loch with rather dark peaty water which holds average loch trout of 8 to 10 ounces. This is a fairly shallow water and the wading is safe in most areas.

Gossa Water
4/302460

This large water is a short, easy walk from the B9071 and is a favourite with a number of local anglers. There are a number of shallow, rocky areas on the road side which can be waded with care. Good quality brown trout averaging 10 ounces which fight well. Good for boats but beware of underwater boulders. Local anglers call this water "Stump".

Housa Water
4/288442

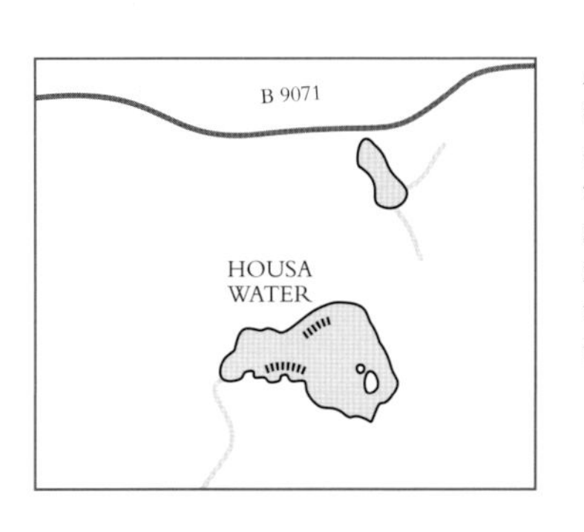

A 15 minute walk south from the road brings you to this dark, dour loch. A rocky shore makes wading unwise and the trout average 10 ounces but there are much larger fish to catch you unawares so stay alert at all times.

Loch of Arg
4/302442

A small, shallow loch which is little fished by local anglers. It holds fish of a 6 ounce average but in recent years a few larger fish of more than a pound have been caught.

Loch of Westerwick
4/283432

This loch is full of 6 ounce trout and is the ideal place for a newcomer to fly fishing to learn the skills. Fish lie close to the shore and wading is not required.

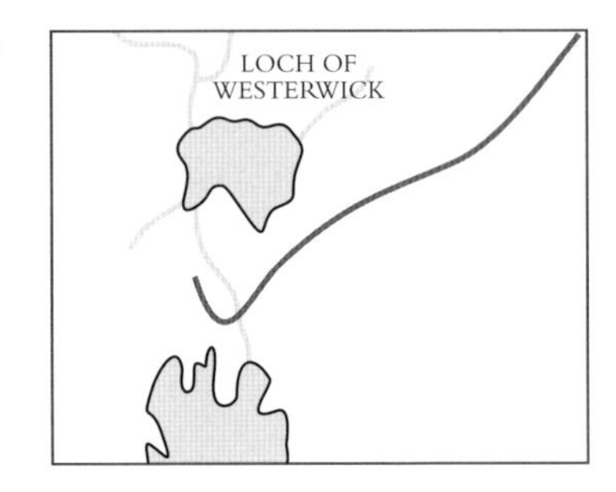

Sand Water
4/262450

Loch of Sotersta
4/262450

Loch of Broch
4/255448

Sand Water is the best of the three with hard-fighting golden trout which average 14 ounces with some to 2 pounds. Clear water and mostly good wading. In Sotersta you can expect good baskets of 6 to 8 ounce trout and further to the west the Loch of Broch is a dark-water loch with average hill-loch trout. Stocked occasionally by SAA.

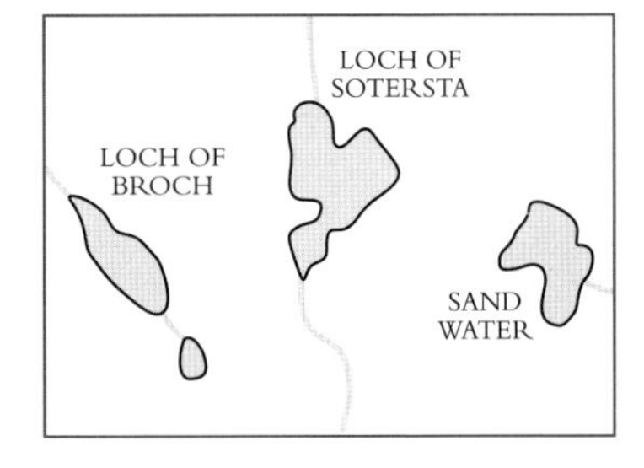

Loch of Semblister
3/337497

Thought to be fishless for many years this loch was stocked by the SAA in 1995 and 1996.

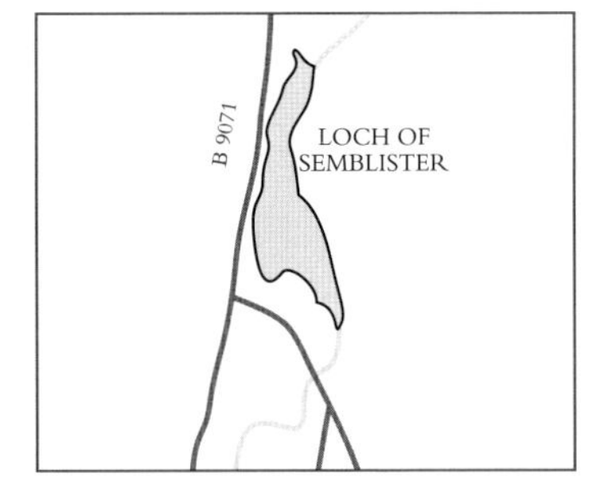

All Whalsay lochs are owned by the Whalsay Angling Association who stock most of the lochs with fry on a regular basis. Visitors can, if they wish, donate to the club's restocking fund by leaving a donation at Tetley & Anderson's shop.

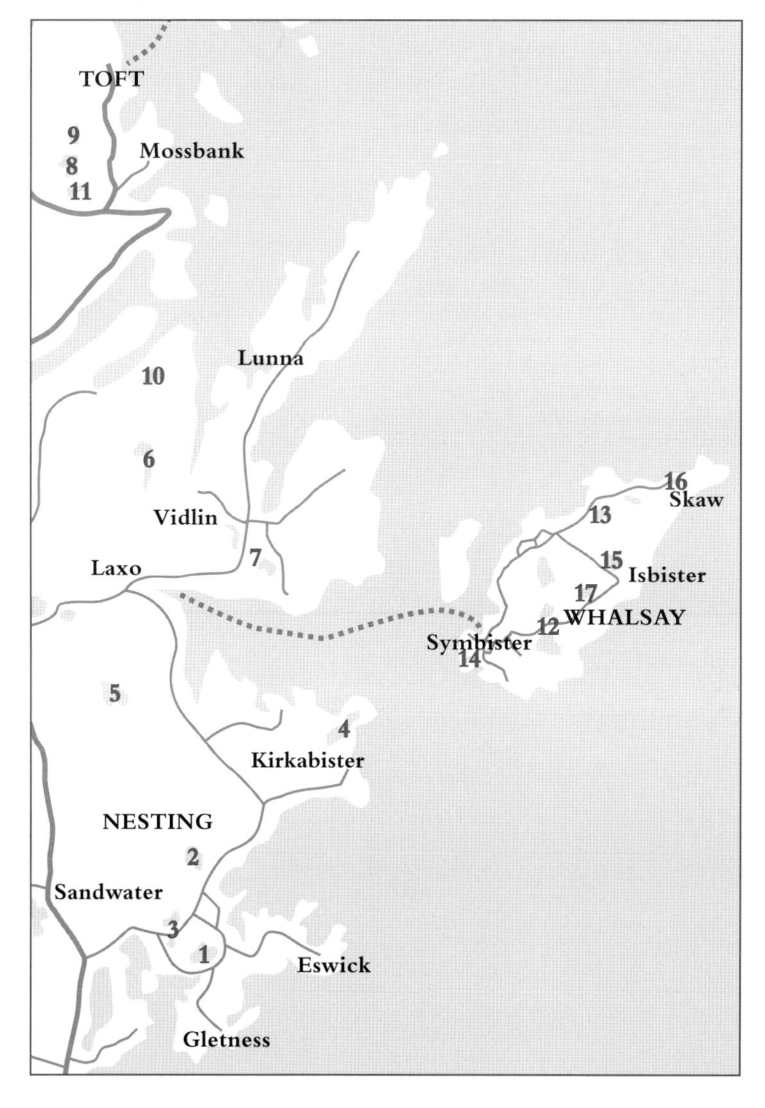

EAST MAINLAND & WHALSAY LOCHS

1 Loch of Benston

2 Loch of Skellister

3 Loch of Freester
Loch of Houlland

4 Loch of Stavaness

5 Gossa Water

6 Laxo Water

7 Burga Water
Kirkhouse Loch

8 Sand Water

9 Neshion Water

10 Mill Loch

11 Loch of Bordigarth

12 Loch of Huxter
Loch of Livister

13 Loch Vats-Houll

14 Loch of Sandwick

15 Loch of Isbister

16 East Loch of Skaw

17 Nuckro Water

Loch of Benston
3/462535

Owned by the SAA this is one of Shetland's premier lochs and many large trout have been taken from this water over the years. They average about a pound but much larger fish are still caught. During the 1997 season at least 40 trout over 3lb were taken from this loch. Wading is safe in most areas and the loch is well-suited to boat fishing. Becomes weedy as the season progresses. There is a size limit of 12 inches on this loch and fish under this size should be returned gently to the water. Good quality brown trout which fight well. The Association has a parking area with boat access to the loch where the burn runs out in the north east bay. Recommended. *Fly fishing only.*

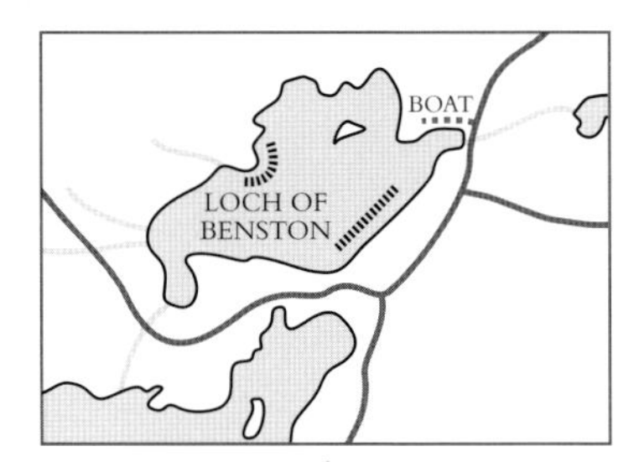

Loch of Skellister
3/460562

Easy access up the rough track which takes you to the north east side of the loch. Deep and sometimes dour, this water has in the past seen fish of 3 pounds and more come to the net, though the average fish is only about 8 ounces.

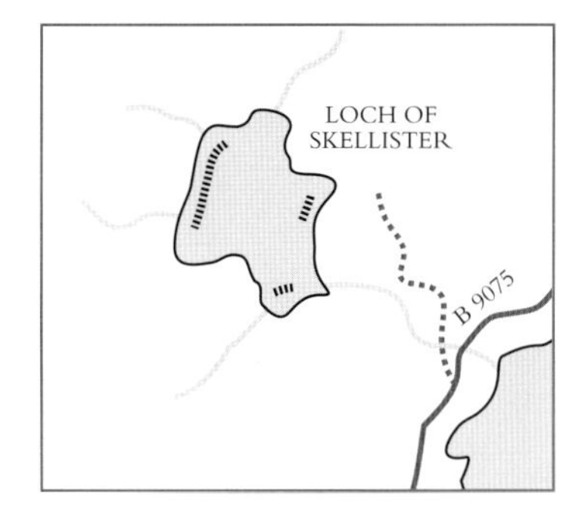

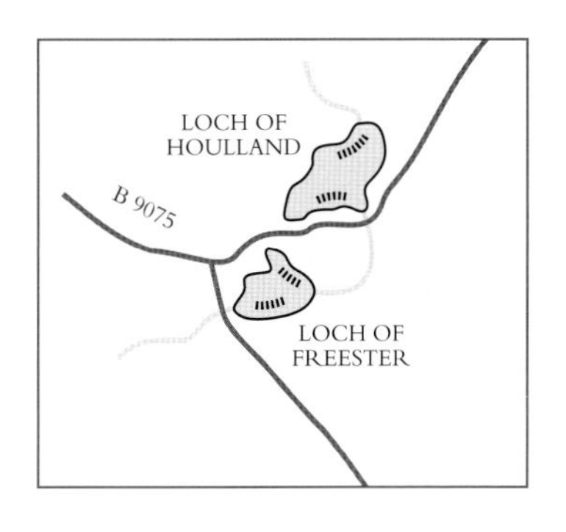

These two small and shallow lochs, which are separated by the south Nesting road, both hold trout of 8 to 12 ounces with the occasional fish over the pound. Both lochs become weedy in places from July on.

Loch of Freester
3/451540

Loch of Houlland
3/455542

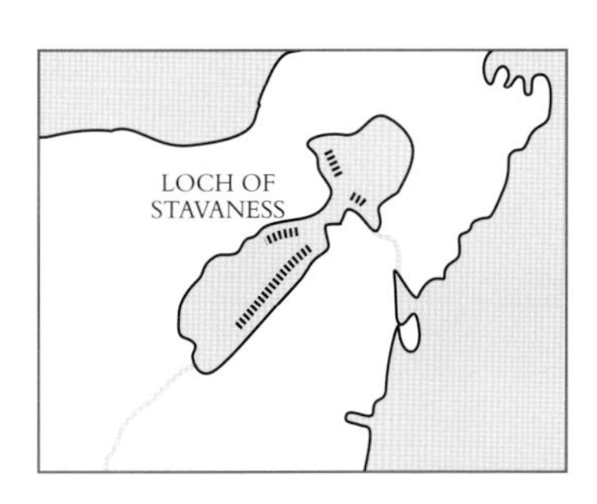

Park at the end of the road at Neap and the loch lies about half a mile over the hill to the north. Brown trout average about 8 ounces with a few fish over the pound. At very high tides the sea can enter the north end of the loch and coalfish can sometimes be caught here in the brackish water. Possibly some sea trout later in the season. Wade the south end only.

Loch of Stavaness
3/500600

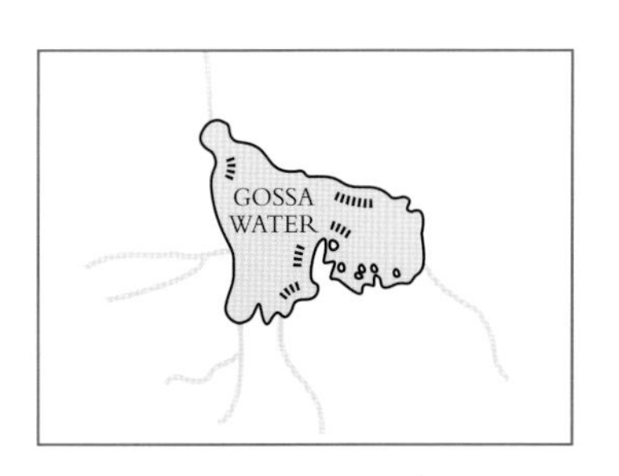

A largish loch which lies up among the hills of North Nesting. A little effort is required to reach this water and the easiest approach is to follow the burn up the hill from the Ayre of Atler until the burn forks then head south west. After high winds the loch becomes very dirty and unfishable. Famous in the past for it's sea trout when fish of 5 or 6 pounds could be expected but sadly the sea trout runs have diminished greatly and the loch is now little fished. The brown trout average 6 ounces.

Gossa Water
3/440606

Laxo Water
3/445650

This loch lies to the north of Laxo at the head of Dury Voe. Follow the right hand branch of the burn northwards for about half a mile and this will bring you to the south end of the loch. Another loch fished in the past for it's run of sea trout but is now populated by mostly small brown trout which average about three to the pound.

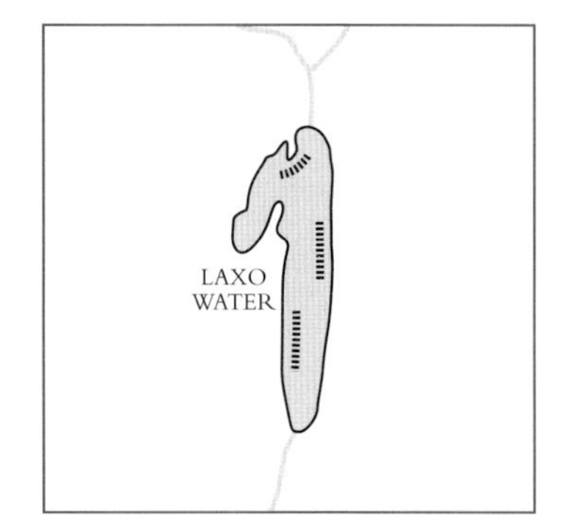

Burga Water
3/481641

A small, shallow water lying west of the Levaneap road and well worth a cast or two. Good quality trout average 10 ounces and wading is mostly safe on a shingly bottom. Some weed patches in the south west corner.

Kirkhouse Loch
3/473650

Shallow and weedy this loch seems to contain mostly small fish.

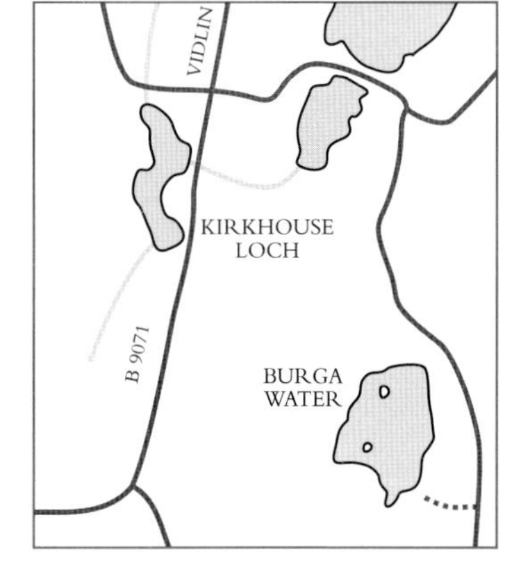

Sand Water
3/423746

This shallow water is said to hold some good fish up to 2 pounds and more but they are not easily caught. Good wading for the most part but the south shore is rocky. Stocked with fry in 1997.

Neshion Water
3/423746

Stocked a few years ago and fish up to 1.5 pounds have been taken. Restocked with fry in 1997.

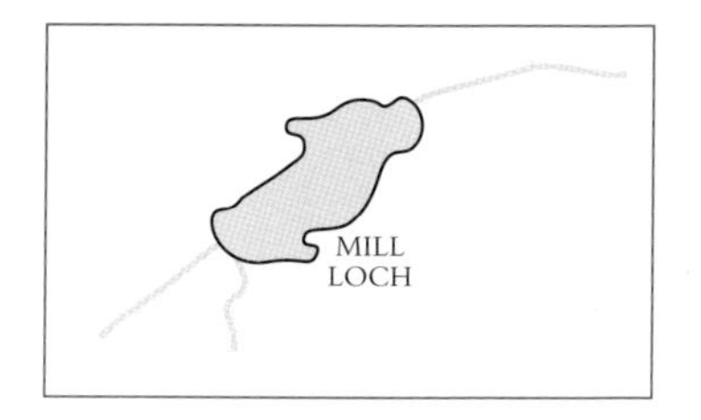

Mill Loch
3/450690

A loch which requires a bit of effort to reach. The easiest way to approach this loch is from the end of the road at Collafirth (430689). Park at the end of the road and then walk up the south east shore of the bay for about half a mile and then bear right up through the shallow depression between the two hills and the loch is straight ahead. Had a reputation in the past for holding large fish up to 6 pounds but now seems to be ignored by most local anglers. The two best areas to fish are the small bay in the south west and the north east end.

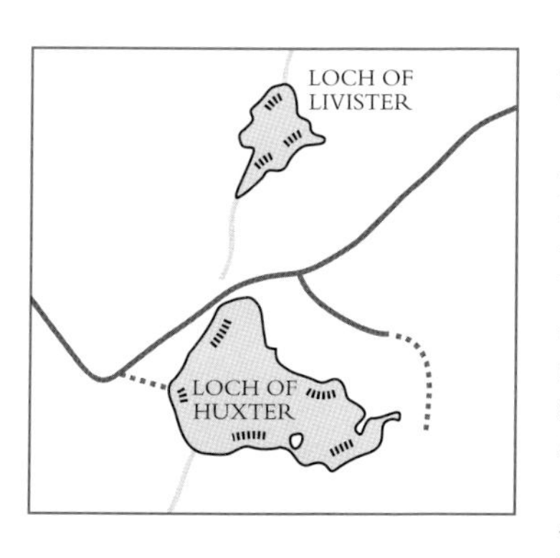

Loch of Huxter
2/558623

A large loch with easy access where the brown trout average 12 ounces but the loch can produce much larger fish - an exceptional fish of 9.5 pounds was caught a few years ago. Wading is awkward except in the south west corner. The best fishing areas are along the south side and in the north east corner.

Loch of Livister
2/558630

A short, easy walk to the north of Huxter this smaller loch can also produce good quality fish to more than 3 pounds. Wading is not necessary and fish lie close to the shore.

Loch Vats-Houll
2/570658

Another loch with easy access from the road with fish of 10 to 12 ounces but be alert for the occasional larger fish which can take you unawares. Slightly coloured water with mainly good wading but beware of slippery stones at the edge. Weeds up from mid-season.

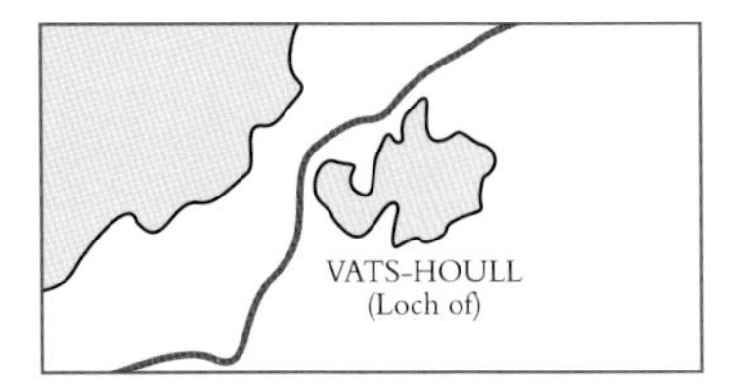

Loch of Sandwick
2/538618

This is the nearest loch to Symbister and holds fish which average 12 ounces with some up to 2 pounds. Wading is difficult and the loch weeds up badly from mid-season.

Loch of Isbister
2/577643

Brown trout average 12 ounces with some fish to more than 2 pounds. Wading is awkward in some places where there is a slippery bottom. Some weed patches in the latter half of the season. Best fishing is to be found on the side nearest the road.

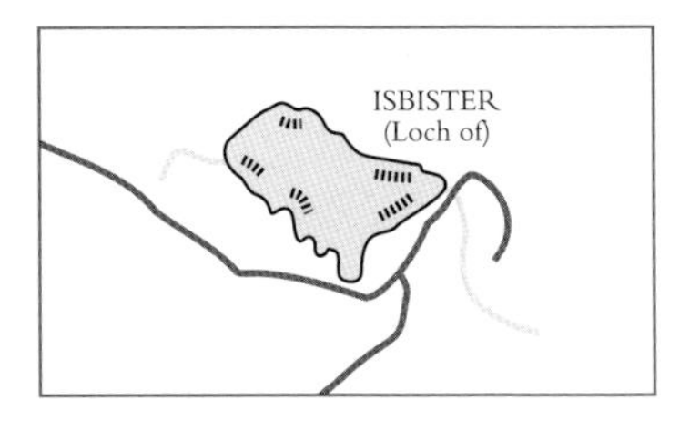

East Loch of Skaw
2/595665

A small, shallow loch lying beside the Whalsay Golf Club's clubhouse at the end of the Skaw road. The fish average 10 to 12 ounces with some fish to 3 pounds. Good wading.

Nuckro Water
2/570635

A very dour loch which can, at times, produce very large fish. Access is very easy but wading is not recommended. The western bay weeds up quickly from early summer onwards.

This part of Shetland offers some of the most rugged scenery in the islands and also a wide variety of fishing ranging from the hill lochs full of small trout to the big-fish waters of Eshaness. There are also the clear water lochs of the Ronas Hill plateau where the angler/walker can find dozens of lochs to choose from.

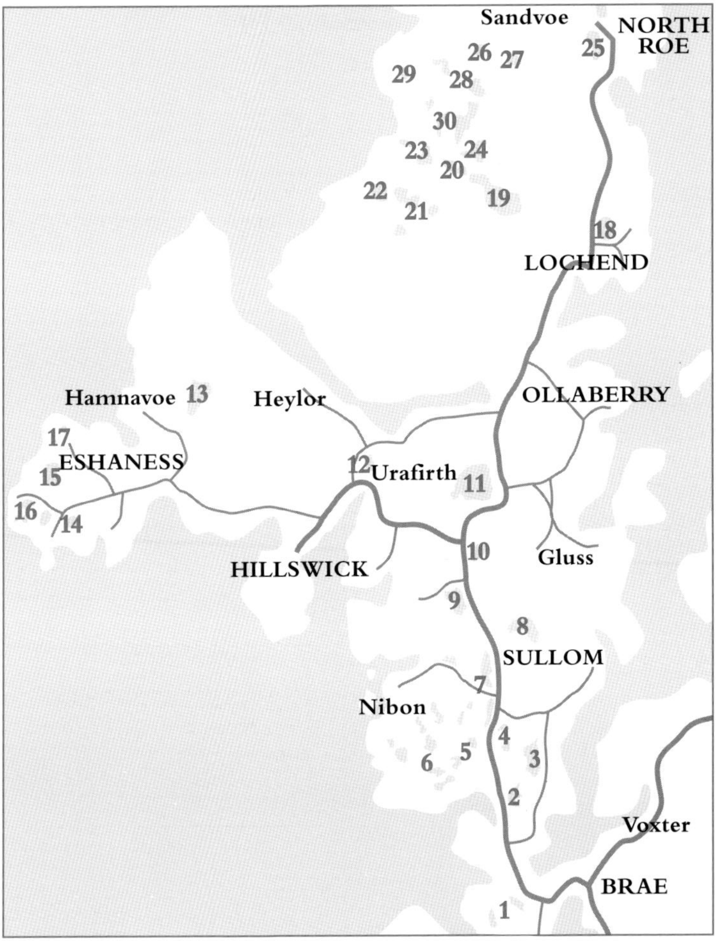

NORTH MAINLAND LOCHS

1 Bays Water
Houlls Water

2 Loch of Haggrister

3 Loch of Lunnister

4 Scora Water
Stanes Water

5 Flagnafield Water
Punds Water

6 Brei Water
Lunga Water
Punds Lochs
Brei Water of Nibon
Lunga Water of Nibon

7 Moora Waters
Johnnie Mann's Loch
Glussdale Water
Trolladale Water

8 Loch of Burraland

9 Punds Water

10 Sandy Lochs

11 Eela Water

12 Loch of Urafirth

13 Gluss Water

14 West Loch
Loch of Breckon

15 Loch of Houlland

16 Loch of Framgord
Loch of Gerdie

17 Loch of Ure
Loch of Leascole

18 Loch of Housetter

19 Roer Water

20 Clubbi Shuns
Maadle Swankie

21 Loch of the Hadd
Many Crooks
Swaabie Water

22 Sandy Water

23 Birka Water
Lang Clodie Loch

24 Tonga Water

25 Loch of Flugarth

26 Mill Loch

27 Pettadale Water

28 Innescord Lochs
Moosa Water

29 Hevdadale Water

30 Muckle Lunga Water
Little Lunga Water
Sae Waters

Bays Water
3/333671

Bays Water is the largest of the two and can be dour at times. It contains good-quality, silvery trout which average about 10 ounces with the occasional fish of more than a pound coming to the net.

Houlls Water
3/340677

Houlls water was stocked in 1997 with fry and this should show results from 2000 onwards.

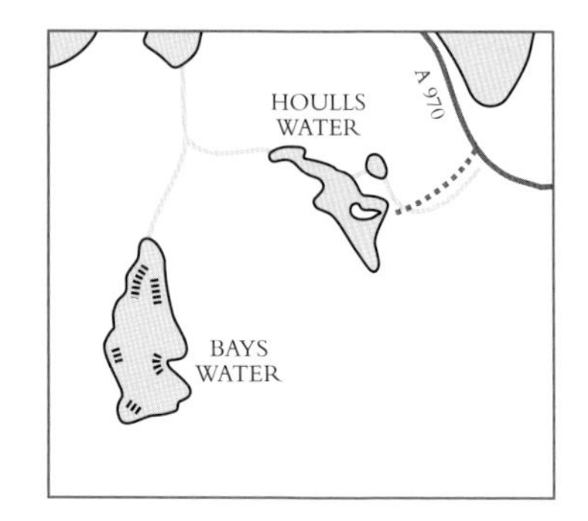

Loch of Haggrister
3/339705

Easy access from the A970 this loch has, in the past, produced fish up to 4 pounds but the average is nearer 12 ounces. There is deep water close to the shore and wading is unwise. Good quality trout in a rugged setting.

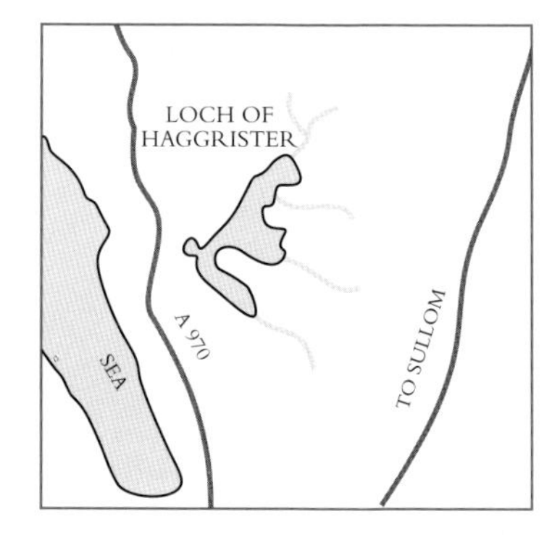

Loch of Lunnister
3/345715

The angling association had a boat on this water many years ago but it is less popular nowadays. There are still some good brownies up to 2 pounds here though the normal size is 10 to 12 ounces. Deep water close to the shore.

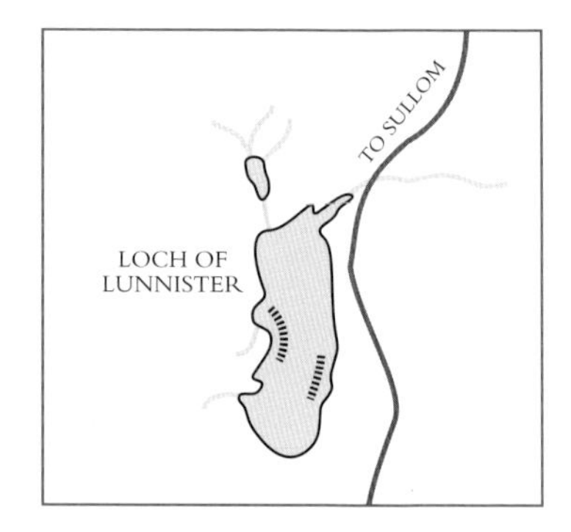

These two small lochs are only a few minutes walk from the road. Scora Water fish average about 10 ounces and are bright and silvery but can be loathe to rise at times. Stanes Water is shallow with some weed patches and the trout are the usual hill-loch trout of 8 to 10 ounces.

Scora Water
3/338720

Stanes Water
3/335721

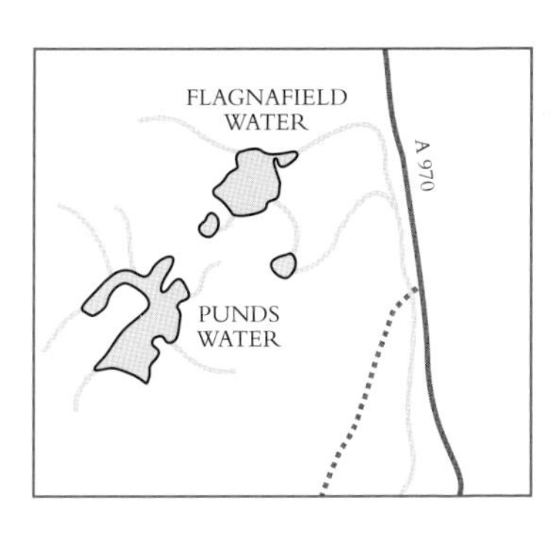

On the other side of the road from the preceding two lochs a ten minute walk up the valley leads you to this clear water loch. Fish of more than 1.5 pounds have been taken here but they are not easy to catch. Becomes quite weedy as the season progresses.

Flagnafield Water
3/329720

Another ten minute walk to the south west brings you to this typical hill loch with trout of 6 to 8 ounces. Some patchy weed from July onwards.

Punds Water
3/325715

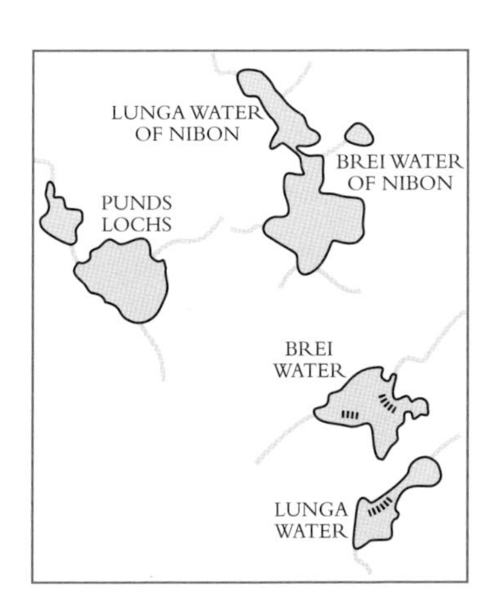

This group of lochs makes for a wonderful day walking and fishing. Travel light and waders are unneccessary. Lunga Water and Brei Water both contain good condition fish of more than 2 pounds but they can be dour, especially the former.
Further to the west and surrounded by hills the Punds Lochs hold good numbers of the normal hill loch trout of 8 to 10 ounces.
The other two, Brei Water of Nibon and Lunga Water of Nibon, are joined by a short burn and both have deep water close to the shore. The trout are mostly about 6 to 10 ounces but there are also some better fish present.

Brei Water
3/320711

Lunga Water
3/320708

Punds Lochs
3/310718

Brei Water of Nibon
3/317719

Lunga Water of Nibon
3/315721

Moora Waters
3/325727

These two waters are said to have been stocked in the past and it is possible that they still contain a few decent fish.

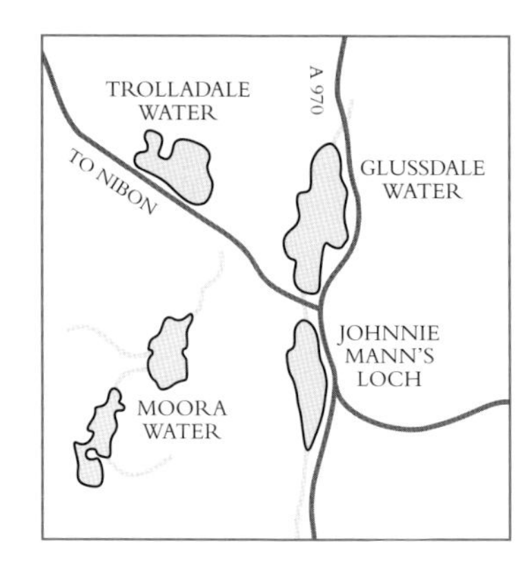

Johnnie Mann's Loch
3/332729

These two roadside lochs have good numbers of mostly small fish of less than 8 ounces and should suit the newcomer to fly-fishing.

Glussdale Water
3/332733

Trolladale Water
3/328735

This small loch lies alongside the narrow road which takes you to Gunnister and can produce trout up to about a pound with most weighing between 6 and 12 ounces. The deepest water seems to be on the road side.

Loch of Burraland
3/340750

A large, shallow loch with a good stock of 6 to 8 ounce fish with the occasional fish over the pound. Becomes very weedy from mid-season. In the past the loch saw good runs of sea trout and there is the possibility of the angler catching one or two sea trout later in the season. The track road to the north of the loch is private.

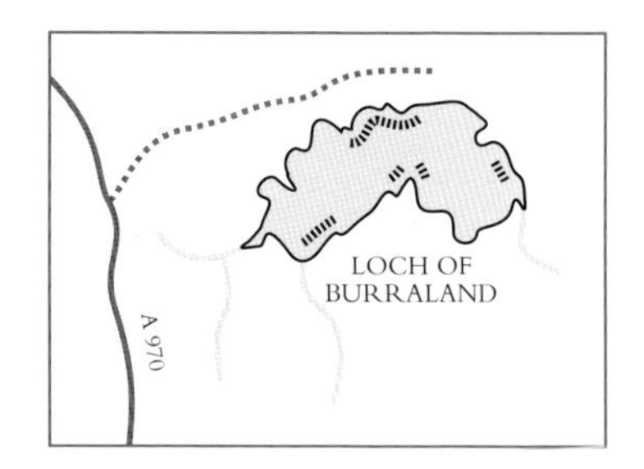

Punds Water
3/327758

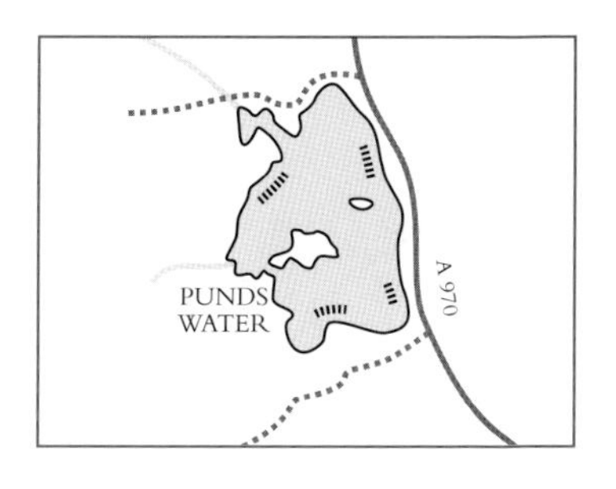

In the past this roadside loch was popular with local anglers and good numbers of trout averaging 12 ounces were caught but in the early 1990's catches dropped and few fish are now caught though the average size has risen and fish of 2 to 3 pounds have been taken. Restocking with fry commenced in 1997 and the results will be watched with interest.

Sandy Lochs
3/328770

These two small lochs hold mainly small fish and wading these lochs is advised against. Both become weedy from mid-season.

Eela Water
3/330788

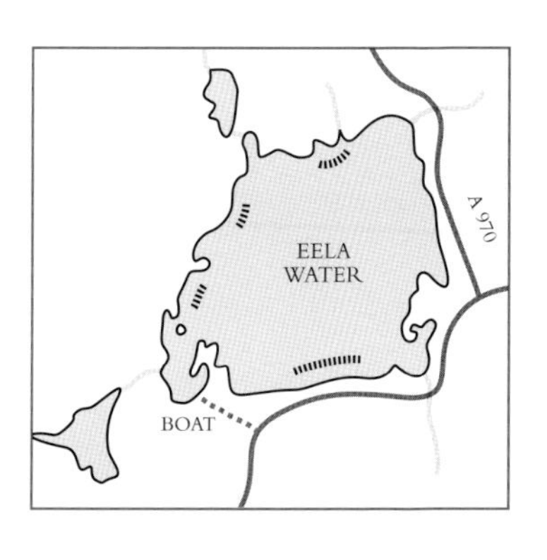

In the past this water had a reputation for large baskets of small trout but during the 1980's increased fishing pressure resulted in an increase in the average weight and this is now about 12 ounces with some fish nearing 2 pounds. Fish can be caught all round the loch and the Association boat is moored in a small bay in the south west corner of the loch. Little Eela water is shallow and weedy and has mostly small fish.

Loch of Urafirth
3/301792

A shallow, coloured water loch with good numbers of small brown trout.

Gluss Water
3/256810

This good-sized loch is shallow and clear with trout of good size. The average is about 12 ounces but there are fish to more than 3 pounds. Trout can be caught all over the loch and there are some excellent fish waiting to be caught. Access by a rough hill road.

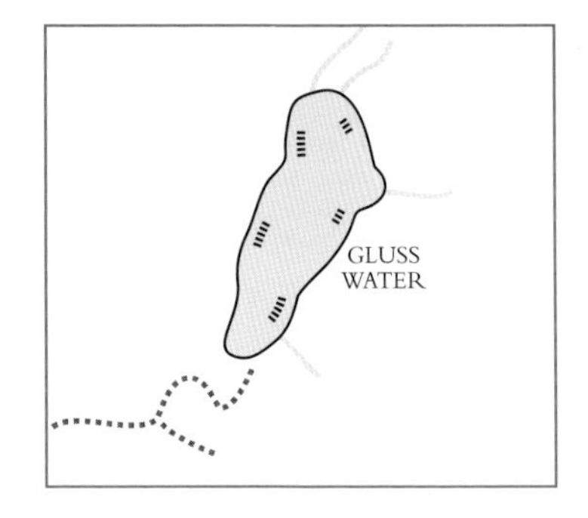

West Loch
3/218780

Small, shallow and weedy this little loch can produce monsters of more than 5 pounds. Best fished early in the season before weed growth becomes excessive. Very dour but well worth an hour or two. Stocked regularly by the SAA.

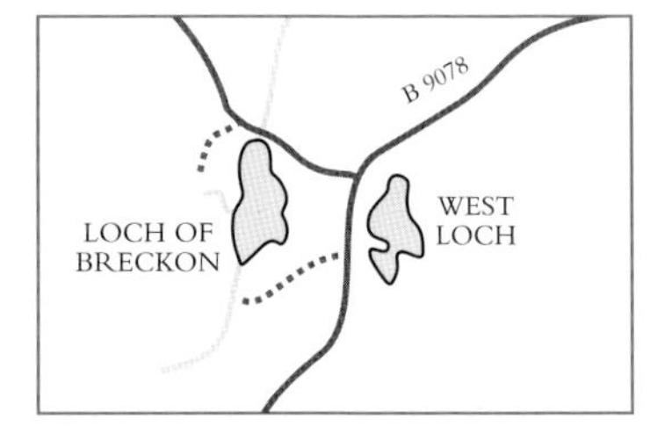

Loch of Breckon
3/214780

Easy access with a good parking area beside the loch. This is another dour water which can produce large fish and in the past fish up to 8 pounds have been caught. Top quality, hard-fighting trout. Stocked by the SAA.

Loch of Houlland
3/215790

A ten minute walk over the low hill on the opposite side of the road from Framgord will bring you to what must be one of the best of Shetland's brown trout lochs. A good number of 2 and 3 pound fish are caught each year and the occasional fish of more than 5 pounds. Fish can be caught all round this shallow loch which is better fished in the first half of the season before the weed becomes too wide-spread.

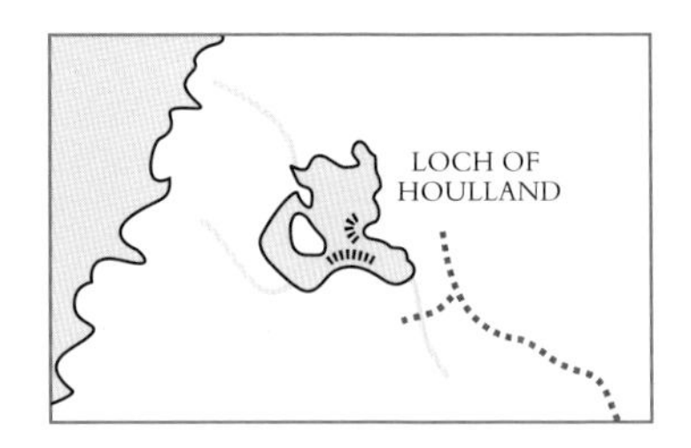

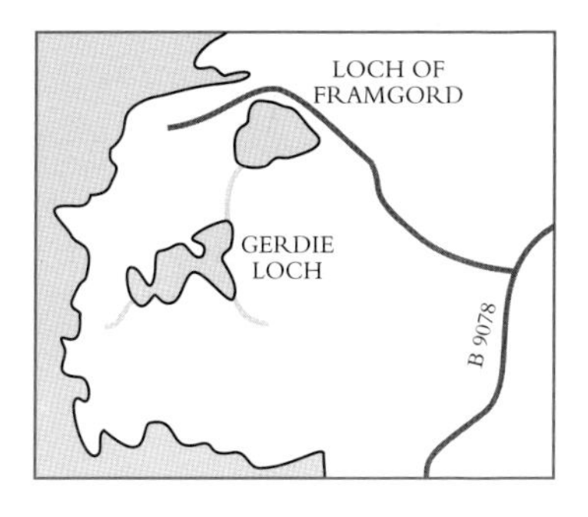

Loch of Framgord
3/210784

This roadside loch lies on top of the hill just before you reach the lighthouse. The water is crystal clear and the loch holds some large fish of more than 3 pounds but they are not easy to catch. Stocked by the SAA.

Loch of Gerdie
3/206780

A few minutes walk south from Framgord will take you to this split loch. The eastern loch is deepest and holds fish of more than 2 pounds while the other shallow loch has produced fish over 7 pounds. Stocked by the SAA.

Loch of Ure
3/218805

Loch of Leascole
3/215800

These two small lochs are an easy 15 minute walk to the north of Houlland. Leascole is shallow and weedy but trout of more than 3 pounds can be caught here. Ure is deeper and is separated from the sea by a boulder beach at the north end where the deepest water can be found. There are some good fish in this loch also but, as with those in Leascole, they are not easy to catch.

Loch of Housetter
1/364853

A shallow, clear water loch which has bright little fish of 4 to 8 ounces with the occasional better fish. Good wading on the east shore. Some weed patches from July onwards.

Roer Water
1/340860

This is the nearest of the large group of lochs to be found in the area known as the "back of Ronas Hill". To cover even a few of these lochs involves quite a long walk and the angler should be well equipped - walking boots, waterproof clothing and map and compass are essential. The easiest route to the loch is to take the steep narrow road which ascends Collafirth Hill. About 300 yards up the road you will see a rough track heading off to your right - park the car here because the track is impassable for normal vehicles but worth checking out for 4X4s. An easy 40 minute walk along the track will bring you to the shore of the loch. Roer Water is a large, deep water with a rocky shore. The trout are bright silvery fish and average 10 ounces with some fish over a pound. In the past there was a boat on the loch when good runs of sea trout entered the loch via the Roerwater Burn. Most of the lochs in this area lie on a hard granite bedrock which results in crystal clear water but a low PH value.

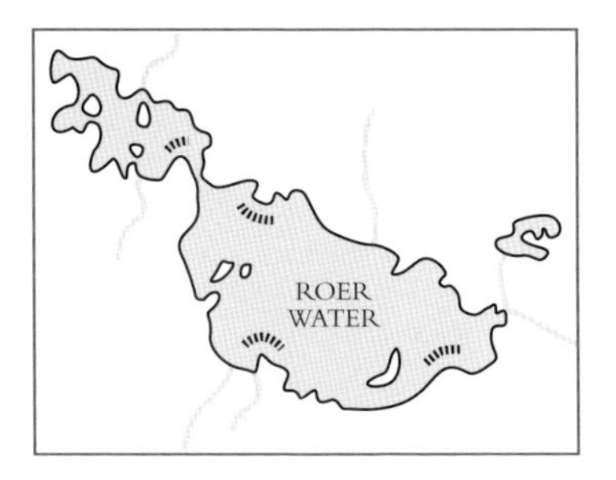

Clubbi Shuns
1/331868

Maadle Swankie
1/327870

Linked to Roer Water by short burns these two waters contain smaller and darker coloured fish which average about three to the pound. There is deep water close to the shore and fish are caught all over.

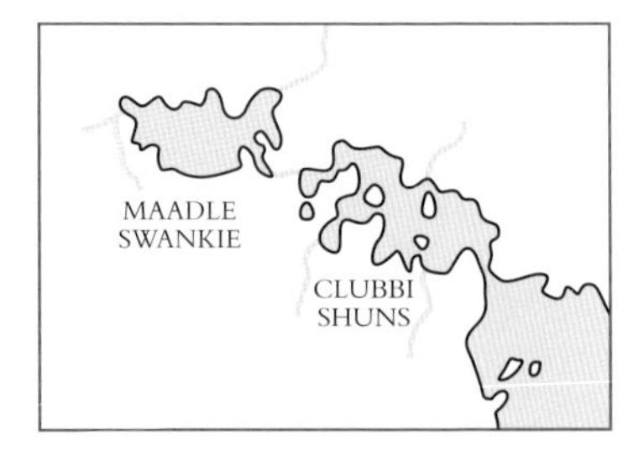

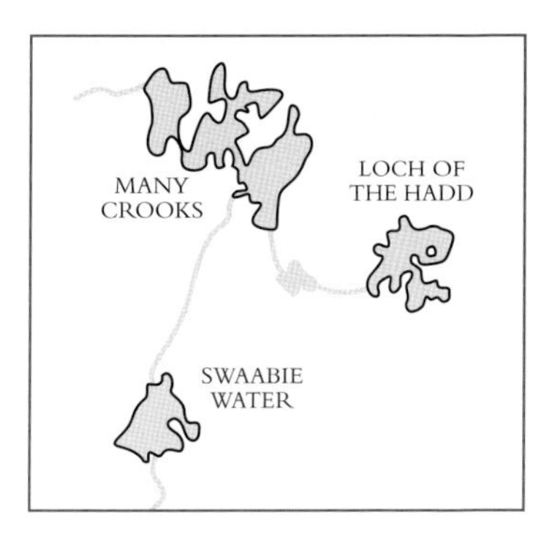

Loch of the Hadd
1/320860

Many Crooks
1/312862

The Loch of the Hadd holds traditional hill-loch trout of about 8 ounces and an average basket would be four to six fish. Many Crooks is a group of three interlinked lochs all of which contain good numbers of trout - most of which seem to be between 6 and 10 ounces.

Swaabie Water
1/310854

One of the remotest waters and one of the most infuriating. This small, shallow loch holds good quality trout of more than 3 pounds but they are hard to catch and a normal basket would contain a few small trout of 8 ounces or smaller. The water is as clear as crystal and there are some excellent trout to be caught.

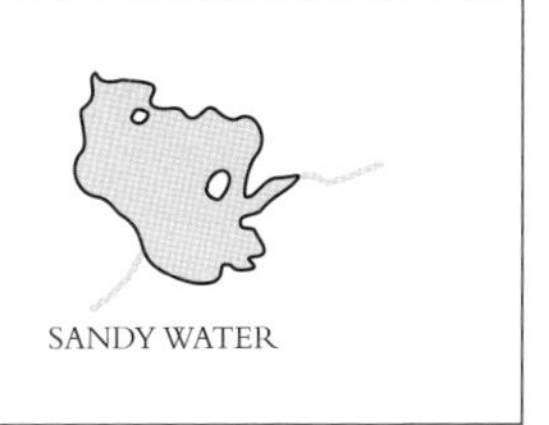

Sandy Water
1/305865

A large clear water loch with a number of small islands. There is deep water close in along much of the rocky shoreline. The trout are bright and silvery, like sea trout, and average 8 to 10 ounces with some better fish up to a couple of pounds. Bank fishing for hard-fighting trout and you are unlikely to be disturbed.

Birka Water
1/318873

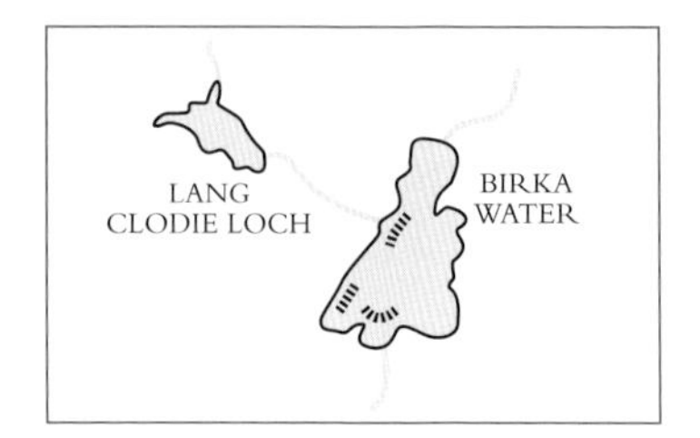

Birka Water is deep for the most part, the north bay being the only shallow area, and trout can be taken all round the loch. They are typical hill-loch trout which average about 8 ounces and there are some fish of more than a pound, so be alert at all times. The Moshella Lochs to the south of Birka Water hold good stocks of mainly small fish.

Lang Clodie Loch
1/311879

If you follow the short, steep burn which flows out of Birka Water westwards you will find one of the most picturesque lochs in Shetland. The Lang Clodie Loch is situated on the grassy cliff-top with an outflow burn which disappears over the cliff edge as a spectacular waterfall. The trout in the loch are mostly small but the occasional fish of a pound or more comes to the net. Remote, but considering the number of lochs in the area, well worth the effort.

Tonga Water
1/332875

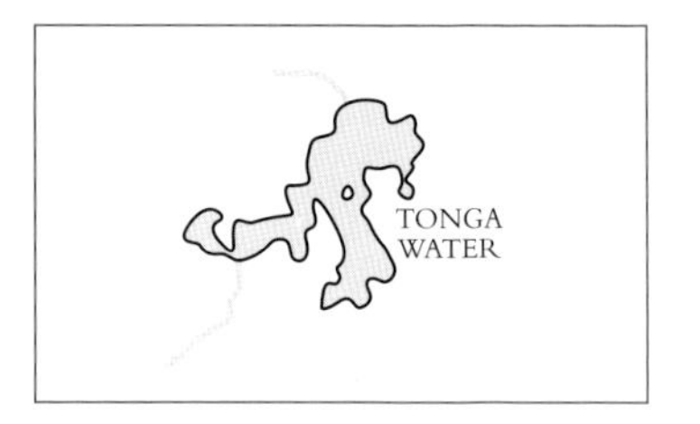

An irregular-shaped loch with many fishy bays and points where a basket of six or eight fish would not be unusual. Most fish are 6 to 10 ounces and are of the typical hill-loch variety.

Loch of Flugarth
1/363902

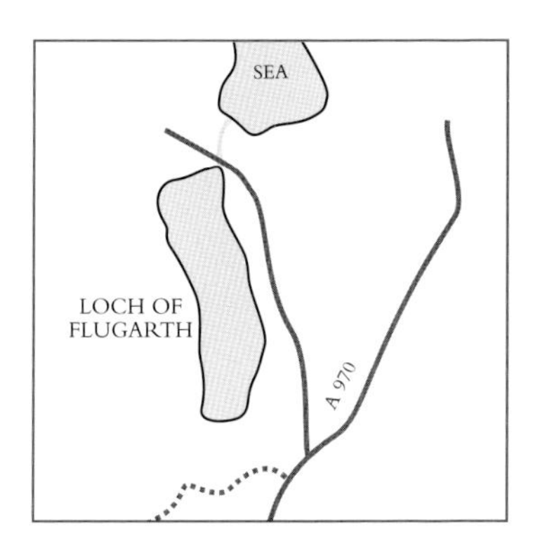

This low-lying water is close to North Roe and lies behind the beach at Sand Voe which was popular for the sea trout which were caught in good numbers from the beach. The fish in Flugarth are small and numerous and most of the loch is easily waded. Easy access and ideal for the beginner.

Mill Loch
1/331900

Deep water close to the shore and can be dour but there are said to be some good fish in the loch. The normal size seems to be 8 to 10 ounces and there are no weeds to hinder the angler.

Pettadale Water
1/341899

The first loch on your right as you go in the track which leaves the A970 at North Roe is just a few minutes walk away. This is a small, shallow water which becomes very weedy in the late season. The water is slightly coloured and wading is not recommended. Trout average 10 ounces with an occasional better fish of a pound or more.

Innescord Lochs
1/322898

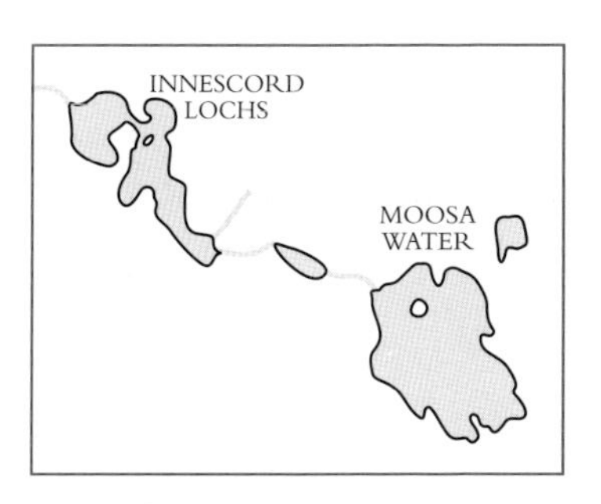

The larger east loch has the better fish and as you would expect are harder to catch. The smaller west loch seems to hold good numbers of fish of the 4 to 6 ounce size and both have a rocky shore with good fishing water close to the margins. Fish of more than 2 pounds have come from the larger loch.

Moosa Water
1/331890

Another deep, dour loch with large fish which rarely rise to the fly but there are good quality fish of more than 3 pounds in the loch.

Hevdadale Water
1/312895

A dour water near Hevdadale Head which can produce the occasional fish of more than 2 pounds but they are not easy to catch.

Muckle Lunga Water
1/330883

There are large fish in this loch but they are rarely caught on the fly. A number are caught on the spinner each year and the average is about 2 pounds.

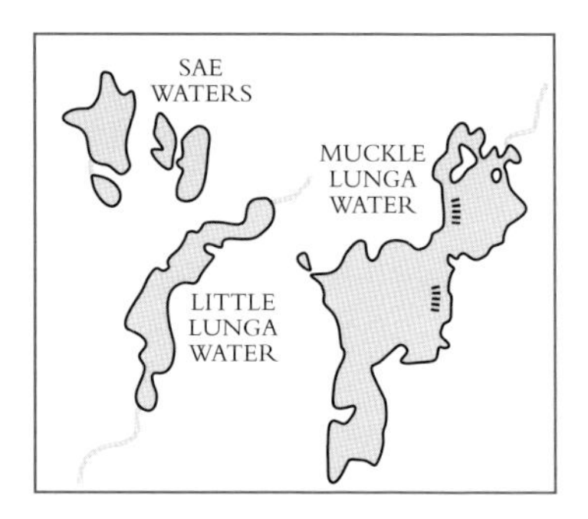

Little Lunga Water
1/320881

Just to the west of Muckle Lunga Water this clear water loch holds silvery fish of about 10 ounces and a few fish up to 2 pounds. A basket of three or four fish would be considered good for this water. No need to wade as there is deep water close to shore.

Sae Waters
1/320888

The largest of these lochs seems to hold fish of 6 to 8 ounces.

YELL LOCHS

Many local anglers prefer to concentrate on Yell for its sea trout fishing and forget about the range of good brown trout fishing which is available. Most of the lochs are easily accessible, apart from the hill lochs in the north western part of the island.

1. Mussel Loch
2. Loch of Ulsta
3. Loch of Littlester
Loch of Kettlester
4. Loch of Vollister
5. Lochs of Lumbister
6. Loch of Brough
7. Loch of Vatsetter
8. Cro Waters

Mussel Loch
2/472790

This small loch lies close to the sea and holds hard-fighting trout of an 8 ounce average. Difficult wading and care should be taken. Anglers should be aware that this loch is in an area of special conservation linked to the protection of otters.

Loch of Ulsta
2/472790

Just a few minute's walk off the B9081 and about a mile north of the ferry terminal at Ulsta this small loch holds mainly small brownies which rise well to the fly. Good bank fishing but the weed becomes a hindrance as the season progresses.

Loch of Littlester
2/511798

Lying by the roadside just west of Burravoe is said to hold better than average trout and in the past has produced fish of more than 4 pounds. Nowadays the trout average 12 ounces with a few fish to 2 pounds. A favourite area to fish is the burn mouth at the east end though good fishing can be had over much of the loch. A clear water loch which should be waded with care. Some weed patches in the late season.

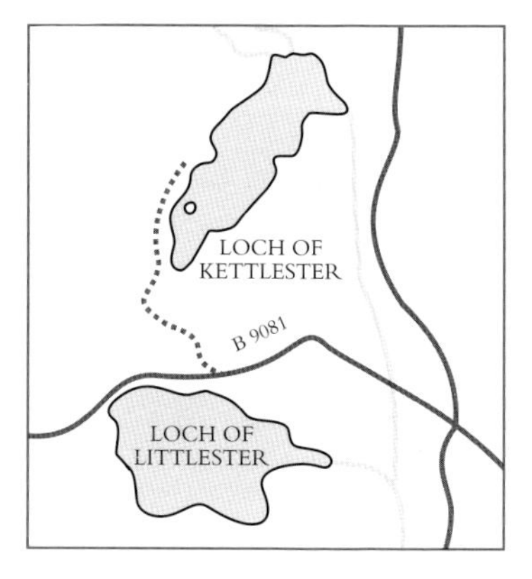

Loch of Kettlester
1/513810

Lying just north of Littlester on the other side of the road holds rather dark coloured fish but there are plenty of them. The average is about 8 ounces but be ready for the occasional better fish. If wading care should be taken.

Loch of Vollister
1/478943

Reaching this loch involves a 1.5 mile walk along the shore of Whale Firth but the effort may be well rewarded. The loch was stocked at the beginning of the century by the Windhouse Estate and good numbers of trout in the 3 to 4 pound range have been caught over the years though the average recently is about 12 ounces but there are still some fish of 2 pounds plus caught. Good wading in most areas except around the burn mouth on the south shore. Owned by the RSPB.

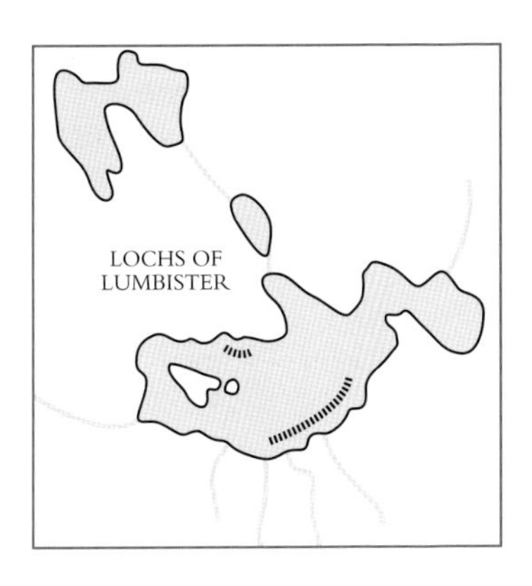

Lochs of Lumbister
1/485967

This group of lochs lie a half hours walk west of the main road. The largest loch has a number of islands and shallows and there is good wading for much of the south shore. The trout in these waters are of a 6 to 8 ounce average with the occasional fish of 1 pound plus. A superb day's fishing for the energetic angler. Owned by the RSPB. The southern boundary of Lumbister is a special area of conservation because of its blanket bog characteristics.

Loch of Brough
1/530030

Has had a good reputation over the years and fish up to 3 pounds have been taken though the average is about 12 ounces. Good bank fishing and one favourite area is the north end. A coloured water loch and wading is neither necessary or advisable.

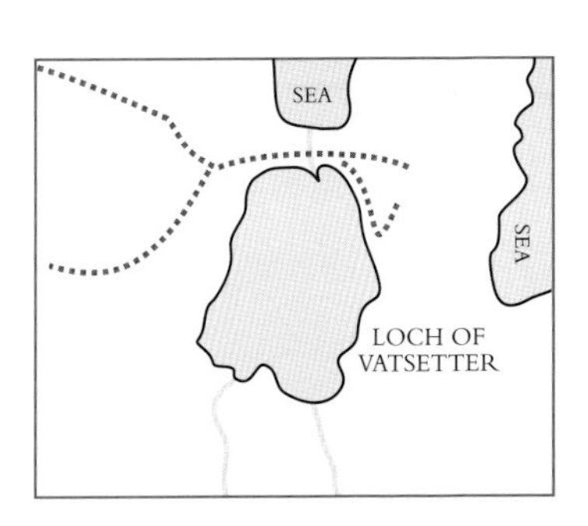

Loch of Vatsetter
1/533890

This loch lies close to the sea and is fished more for the sea trout which run the short burn than for the brown trout which are small. Good wading at the north end where there is a sandy bottom. Some weed patches later in the year.

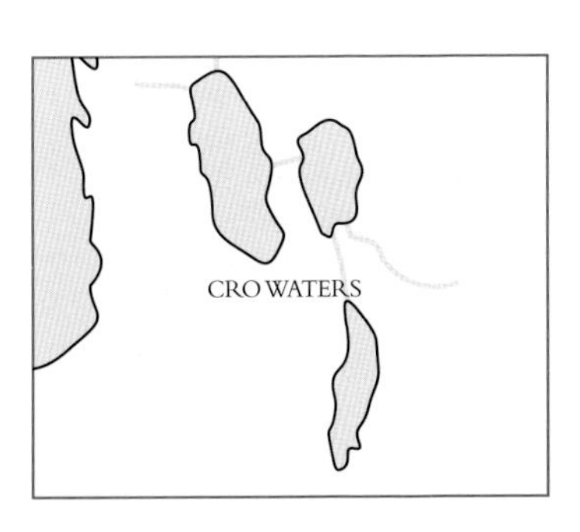

Cro Waters
1/450940

A group of lochs to the west of Grimister on the west side of the island which hold some good fish. The south loch is deep and weedy in places and has produced fish up to 3 pounds 8 ounces. Has a black rocky bottom.

FETLAR LOCHS

Compared to other areas of Shetland, Fetlar has relatively few lochs. However, these lochs contain good trout and a visit to the island is recommended. Large areas of the island are classified as a bird reserve and anglers should therefore cause as little disturbance as possible.

1 **Papil Water**

2 **Skutes Water**

3 **Loch of Winyadepla**

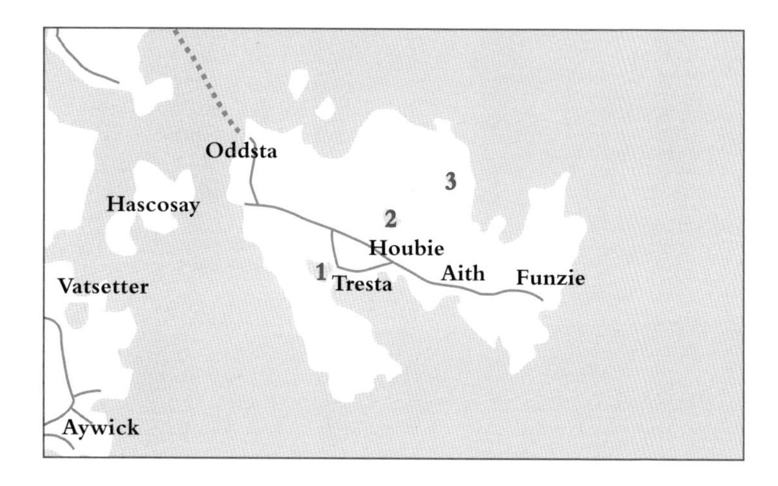

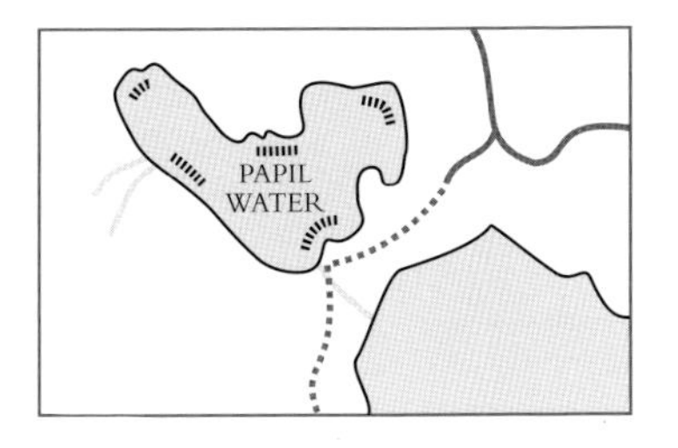

The most popular loch on the island with good quality brown trout of 10 to 12 ounces average though fish up to 4 pounds have been taken. Easy access and good bank fishing with some excellent trout waiting to be caught. Some weed patches from mid-season and there is a chance of a few sea trout entering the loch on a high tide from September onwards.

Papil Water
1/605905

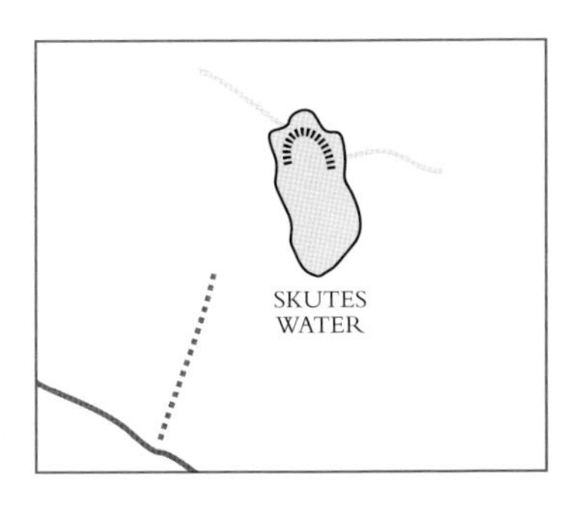

Good quality golden-bellied fish of 10 to 12 ounces are to be caught here. Good wading on a hard bottom. The loch is situated in a bird reserve, so please do not disturb nesting birds.

Skutes Water
1/623918

A long walk of about 2 miles is required to reach this remote loch which has a reputation for being dour. The numbers of trout are small but they make up for that in size and fish up to 4 pounds have been caught. Easily fished from the shore but wade with caution. Again be aware that access to the loch is through a bird reserve and therefore care for wildlife is necessary.

Loch of Winyadepla
1/640930

UNST LOCHS

The Unst Angling Club are asking visiting anglers to pay a £5 annual membership fee on a voluntary basis. The proceeds of this shall go towards restocking the Unst lochs. The club is also asking visiting anglers to keep only four fish (12" or over). The club has a boat for hire on the Loch of Cliff at a charge of £5 per session. The proceeds of the boat hire goes towards the restocking scheme. Further details from "Rod & Line", Harbour Street, Lerwick.

1 Loch of Snarravoe

2 Loch of Stourhoull

3 Loch of Watlee

4 Loch of Cliff

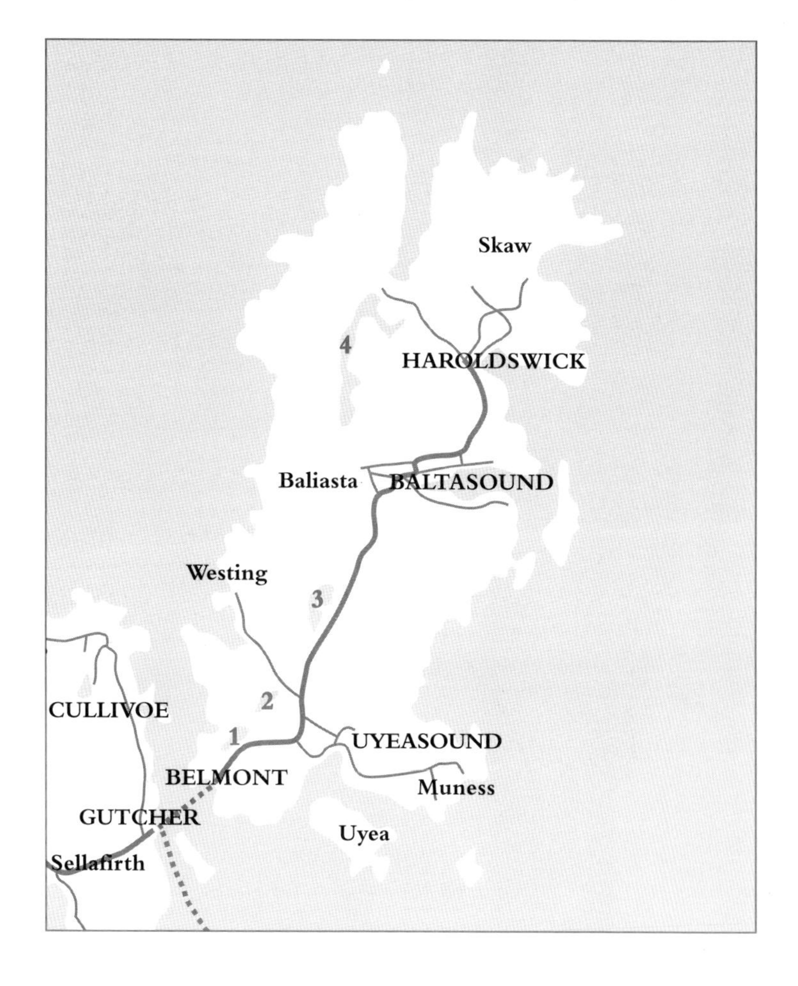

Loch of Snarravoe

1/570015

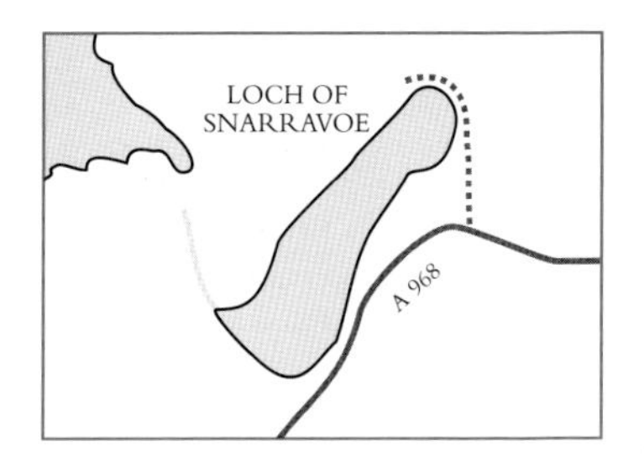

There is easy access from the A968 and this loch is well worth an hour or two. The water is clear as crystal and the trout caught here are golden in colour and fight well. The fish have a high average weight of 14 ounces with some to 3 pounds. Generally safe wading.

Loch of Stourhoull

1/580028

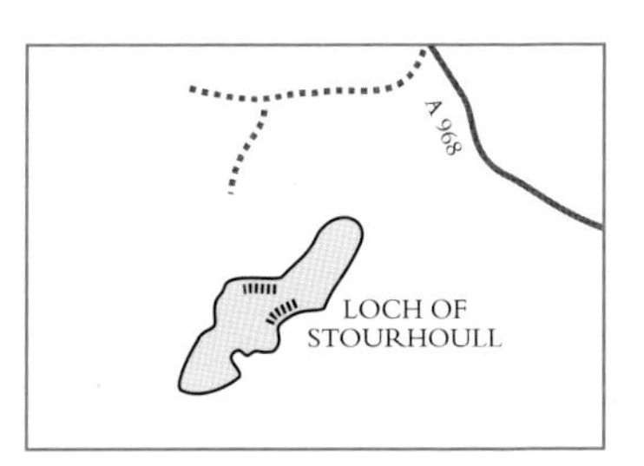

A loch with a reputation for being dour that has, in the past, produced hard-fighting trout up to 4 pounds. Again, crystal-clear water and some weed beds begin to show from mid-season.

Loch of Watlee

1/593050

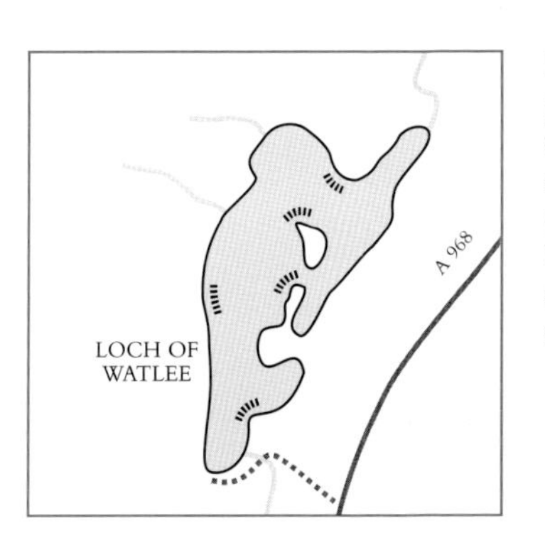

Easy access via the track to the pumping station at the south end of the loch. Brown trout average 10 ounces with fish to 2 pounds or more. Care should be taken when wading and some areas weed up. Good fishing around the island.

Loch of Cliff
1/600120

This, the longest loch in Shetland, has had for many years the reputation of holding small and numerous brown trout. The size and quality of the fish has now improved considerably and the average is about 10 ounces with a number of fish over 2 pounds taken each season. The loch is easily approached at either the north or south end. The loch also recieves a run of sea trout via the burn at the north end. Good for boat fishing though parts of the loch weed up from mid-summer. A boat is available for hire through the Baltasound Hotel.

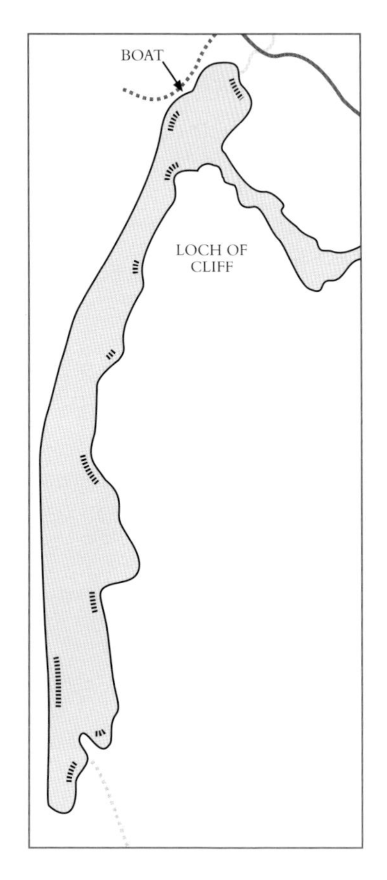

FISHING RECORD

DATE	LOCH	WEATHER	No. OF FISH	WEIGHT	COMMENTS

Fishing record

DATE	LOCH	WEATHER	No. OF FISH	WEIGHT	COMMENTS

Fishing record

DATE	LOCH	WEATHER	No. OF FISH	WEIGHT	COMMENTS

FISHING RECORD

DATE	LOCH	WEATHER	No. OF FISH	WEIGHT	COMMENTS